How to Start a Business and Ignite Your Life

A Simple Guide to Combining Business Wisdom with Passion

How to Start a Business and Ignite Your Life

A Simple Guide to Combining Business Wisdom with Passion

Ernesto Sirolli, PhD

SQUAREONE
PUBLISHERS

Sirolli Institute®, Enterprise Facilitation®, and Trinity of Management® are registered trademarks of the Sirolli Institute.

COVER DESIGNER: Jeannie Tudor
EDITOR: Colleen Day
TYPESETTER: Gary A. Rosenberg

Square One Publishers
115 Herricks Road
Garden City Park, NY 11040
(516) 535-2010 • (877) 900-BOOK
www.squareonepublishers.com

Library of Congress Cataloging-in-Publication Data

Sirolli, Ernesto.
 How to start a business and ignite your life / Ernesto Sirolli.
  p. cm.
 Includes bibliographical references and index.
 ISBN 978-0-7570-0374-5
 1. New business enterprises—Management. 2. Entrepreneurship. I. Title.
  HD62.5.S574 2012
  658.1'1—dc23

                          2012011072

Printed in the United States of America

10 9 8 7 6 5 4 3 2 1

Contents

This book is dedicated to Martha.
I couldn't have done it without you!

Acknowledgments

I owe a debt of gratitude to all the entrepreneurs whom I have met over the past twenty plus years. They have taught me everything I know about business, and so much about life. Maurice Green, John Totterdel, David Leith, Kevin and Christine Inkster, and Steve and Karin Birbeck, among many others, have inspired me with their entrepreneurial spirit. Thank you.

The Enterprise Facilitators I have trained worldwide are too many to acknowledge individually, but their collective work continues to prove that passion and intelligence have no geographical limit. I salute and thank them for being so committed to helping people do what they love to do, and do it beautifully. They have enabled individuals in poor communities all over the world to make a living, feed their families, and employ others, in turn supporting the local economies. Brian Willoughby, Micko O'Byrne, Neville Forman, Suzette McFaul, Linda McCowan, Fabrice Ilunga Mujinga, Rubina Khan, Bryn Hackland, Moe Forouzan, I sincerely thank you and your colleagues in Australia, New Zealand, the United States, Canada, the Democratic Republic of the Congo, and Great Britain. You are "family doctors of business" who are extraordinary at your jobs, and who treat your work as its own reward. As Myron Kirkpatrick once said, "This is the best job I have ever had."

I am indebted to my late father, Dr. Francesco Sirolli, who taught me the central role that the family doctor can play in the lives of those around him, and who inspired me in my efforts to help others. I remember taking walks with my father as a child through the village of Altino, Italy, passing farmhouses surrounded by grapevines and shaded by fig trees. Sometimes, a farmer or two would emerge from a barn or orchard, curious about the man and child walking on the sun-drenched road. Recognizing my father, their faces would light up, and they would call out his name, Don Franco. He would reply affectionately by calling them by their local nicknames. At times, these men and women would take my father's hand or touch his arm, and tell stories about how he had saved the life of one of their family members or friends, whether from a terrible illness, an accident, or a difficult birth. They wanted me to know what my father had done for them, and the difficult times they had shared or through which he had helped them. I walked away from these encounters feeling proud of my father and, despite my young age, knowing the kind of man that I wanted to be one day.

I also want to offer my sincere thanks to the team at Square One Publishers who helped make this book possible. My publisher, Rudy Shur, rescued me from forever reworking the manuscript. Richard Mintzer helped me with language and content, and my editor, Colleen Day, kept me on track. Without the three of them, I would still be writing Chapter 1.

Finally, and most important, I would like to thank my wife and traveling companion, Martha, to whom this book is dedicated. Without her efforts and continued support, it would have been impossible for me to tackle a task as demanding as this book--as well as my first book, running the Sirolli Institute, constant traveling, my family life, and my general health and peace of mind. Thank you, Martha. I will take you to Paris one of these days.

A Word About Gender

In an effort to avoid awkward phrasing within sentences, it is our publishing style to alternate the use of generic male and female pronouns according to chapter. When referring to a "third-person" entrepreneur, odd-numbered chapters will use male pronouns, while even-numbered chapters will use female pronouns.

Preface

The single most important question to ask any aspiring entrepreneur is: What do you love to do? After all, how can a person commit time, money, and energy to a business endeavor if it is not something he or she loves? Some people may take issue with the word "love," because it seems inappropriate to apply in a business context. So let's use the word passion instead. This term is appropriate to use when talking about entrepreneurship, as it comes from the Latin word meaning "to suffer." And as you may know already, the road to success involves some degree of suffering. Entrepreneurs must endure many trials and tribulations, and it takes passion to overcome them and ultimately triumph. So now I ask you: What is your passion?

If you cannot answer this question right now, you will after reading this book. Knowing your passion is the first step towards finding a line of work that utilizes your strengths and fulfills you. It was my own passion for people and helping others that led me to work with entrepreneurs. My family background and professional experience instilled in me the absolute belief that all people are truly capable of great things, no matter what their personal circumstances may be. Working around the world, I learned that there is no geography to passion and no geography to intelligence. Talented individuals are everywhere. What moved me to help people, though, was not their potential to succeed, but their struggles to succeed. I witnessed the frustration and the despair of entrepreneurs who were trying to establish viable businesses with long-term profitability and growth. I couldn't help but feel compelled to assist them in achieving the success they dreamed of.

I founded the Sirolli Institute, an organization dedicated to helping entrepreneurs and communities establish and expand businesses using a methodology I call Enterprise Facilitation®. Over the last three decades, some 300 communities around the world have used our services. We have worked with countless entrepreneurs to start and retool their companies, create jobs, and stimulate and sustain local economies. We have trained Enterprise Facilitators and Trinity of Management practitioners to carry out this work, and we effectively teach aspiring entrepreneurs how to transform their ideas and passions into successful businesses. We believe our mission is an important one, as entrepreneurship shapes our world and epitomizes the optimism, confidence, and drive needed to surmount the economic challenges that we face. Entrepreneurs are remarkable individuals; they see opportunities where others see only problems, and they should be respected, celebrated, and supported. Where would we be without their passion and vision?

Entrepreneurs offer a glimmer of hope, and their inspiring work offers the possibility of a brave new world. You need only remember the sincere outpouring of sorrow at the passing of Steve Jobs in 2011 to realize that our society stands in awe of great entrepreneurs. Time and time again, they have demonstrated an ability to reinvent not only the economy, but also our way of life. I believe it is crucial to help entrepreneurs succeed because they are the engine of the economy.

I once believed that governments, non-governmental organizations (NGOs), universities, churches, and other well-meaning organizations played just as important a role as entrepreneurs in shaping the economy. In fact, I worked for an NGO in Africa from 1971 to 1977, and was convinced that we could motivate people to adopt the technologies that we had developed in our universities. I believed that the problems of the world could be solved with the "enlightened" guidance of experts, and that economies could be stimulated from the top down. How wrong I was. My own experience working in Zambia, Kenya, Somalia, Algeria, and the Ivory Coast was devastating. Every single new business project failed to sustain itself and, very often, we introduced practices and technologies that were inappropriate and damaging. Ultimately, our efforts did not help the local people.

The same was true for similar volunteer agencies and programs aimed at stimulating local economies and providing aid. Although well-meaning, these ill-conceived programs had the same poor results. Instead of helping people do what they passionately loved to do, we were paying them to do what we wanted them to do. As soon as the program funding ended, the local townspeople would return to doing things exactly as they had been doing them before we arrived. This approach of imposing our ideas on local people hasn't exactly disappeared since my work during the mid-1970s.

Profoundly disillusioned by what I had witnessed, I enrolled in a doctoral program in economics. I became inspired by the work of two prominent thinkers, the economist Ernst Schumacher and Carl Rogers, a psychologist. Although they come from two very different disciplines, their philosophical approaches to people overlap and can be summed up with three key principles, all of which apply to business:

- Help only those who wish to be helped.

- Shut up and listen—find out why you have been invited.

- Remove obstacles to success.

These simple ideas significantly shaped my business philosophy, as well as my approach to helping entrepreneurs, which can be easily summed up as "learning how to shut up." At that point, I set out to do the complete opposite of my experience in Africa, where we were constantly telling people to do what we wanted them to do—and it never worked!

After completing my doctoral degree, I received a scholarship to pursue my research in Western Australia, where I set up my first project demonstrating "responsive development" as a case study for my dissertation. Responsive development means addressing the specific needs and goals of the individuals within a community rather than imposing them. My supportive university supervisor, Professor Peter Newman, provided an introduction, and I was invited to apply my responsive approach to local economic development in a small, isolated rural town in Western Australia called Esperance.

It was a difficult economic time for Esperance. When I arrived, the community was in the midst of an agricultural recession, and unemployment was on the rise. Out of a population of less than 10,000, nearly 500 people—including 34 percent of young people—were unemployed. The fishing industry was also on the decline. A diminishing tuna quota plus diminishing fishing stocks had put the industry in a recession. Most fishermen had gone out of business, and the ones who remained were deeply in debt. This dismal economic climate posed a challenge, but I knew there were people with dreams and ideas, and I was determined to find them. I wanted to help these individuals turn their intelligence and passion into rewarding, successful businesses and reinvent the local economy.

I found my first client, Mauri, within four days. Mauri had once been the manager of a fish-processing factory—the largest company in Esperance—but had lost his job when the industry crashed. He had attempted to start his own business by processing and selling smoked fish out of his garage, but was ultimately shut down by the local health inspector for failing to meet the minimum requirements. Broke, Mauri had joined the ranks of the unemployed. When I met him, he was a frustrated failed entrepreneur who lacked the resources necessary to transform his vision into an operable business and escape poverty.

I explained my purpose for being in Esperance, and Mauri's face lit up instantly. We agreed that I would help him start his business, and he would introduce me as the person who had helped him. Immediately, we went to work to accomplish three things:

1. **Test the product.** I wanted to confirm that Mauri did, in fact, know what he was doing when it came to producing smoked fish—and he did. As soon as I tasted his smoked salmon, I knew that there was no problem with his product. It was the best smoked fish I had ever tasted in my life.

2. **Assess the sales potential of the product.** Mauri and I met with several chefs from some of the best restaurants in Perth, the capital

city of Western Australia. Orders started to fly in for his fish, confirming that there was a strong market demand.

3. **Fund the business start-up.** I helped Mauri apply for a $4,000 loan from a microlending organization. With that small amount of money, Mauri was able to rent a commercial property to relocate production of his smoked fish.

Mauri also employed a couple of people to help him supply smoked fish to some of the trendiest restaurants in the region. The business seemed to be stable, and I thought my job was done. But I soon discovered that Mauri had more trouble coming to him, as angry creditors began calling to complain about unpaid bills. Mauri, meanwhile, had just bought himself a new car. It was then that I realized that the true obstacle to his success was his complete ignorance about financial matters. Fortunately, he did not put up a fight when I suggested asking his accountant to manage the business's finances and become a co-signatory of the company checkbook. With his passion and keen understanding of financial management, the accountant quickly helped Mauri turn his bleak financial picture into a profitable one. As an additional benefit, Mauri was able to commission a sales and marketing company that specialized in selling high-quality seafood to restaurants and catering businesses. Now he had an excellent product, a means of marketing it, and a competent financial manager to deal with all the monetary aspects of the business. Mauri's company flourished, and when Queen Elizabeth visited Australia in 1986, it was his Esperance Smoked Tuna that was served at the royal banquet.

I found my next group of clients at the celebration for the official launch of Mauri's business. I was approached by Peter, one of the five remaining tuna fishermen in Esperance. Suffering from the drastic cut in the tuna quota imposed by the Australian government, Peter was clinging to a livelihood that he loved but had little chance of keeping for much longer. He watched the decline of his industry in bitter isolation, as the five fishermen had not banded together to work towards a solution. After I met Peter, he spoke to the four other tuna fishermen separately and suggested a joint meeting with me. Unfortunately, they shook their heads at the idea and made it clear that nothing short of a miracle would get them to work together. But after a month of refusing, they finally realized that they stood a greater chance of succeeding if they joined forces. They agreed to a meeting.

I first recommended that the fishermen hire someone to conduct market research and find additional markets for their tuna, as they had been selling only to one cannery that monopolized the local industry. It was particularly important to find out if there was a Japanese market, since southern bluefin tuna is highly sought after for sushi and sashimi. A friend of a friend, David, agreed to do this task for a small fee. He then agreed to do future marketing work for the company on a commission basis. Next, we found an English-speaking sushi chef who was willing to visit Esperance and give the fishermen a lesson in how to prepare sashimi. Finally, it was imperative that they employ a qualified individual to act as CFO for their business. As it turned out, the wife of one of the fishermen was a certified public accountant who had been working at the local bank for the past seventeen years. She agreed to step into the financial manager role.

Nine months later, the fishermen were selling their tuna in Tokyo at the famous Tsukiji fish market. A new factory was built in Esperance for processing and packing fresh tuna to meet Japanese sashimi standards. During the following fishing season, 140 tons of tuna was air-freighted to Japan, where it was sold at auction for an average of $7.50 a pound—a world of difference from the 30 cents per pound that the fishermen had been receiving from the Australian cannery. By forming a team and expanding their market, the fishermen were able to remain in the industry that they loved.

We all had big smiles on our faces that fishing season. Mauri's Esperance Smoked Tuna company and the fishermen's Esperance Sashimi Development company became the "good news" items in the West Australian media. The passion of Mauri and the fishermen had paid off, but the lesson to be learned from their stories is not just that there are smart, passionate people in Esperance—that was a given from the start. Rather, the lesson here is twofold. First, my Esperance experience teaches that entrepreneurs can be guided to success if you listen to them carefully, identify the obstacles holding them back, and then work with them to remove these impediments. Second, and perhaps more important, the experience demonstrates that success is possible when entrepreneurs find a team and make sure the three basic areas of business—product, marketing, and financial management—are beautifully looked after.

I noticed a pattern in how Mauri and the fishermen ultimately got their businesses to succeed. Mauri was a passionate individual with a high-quality and marketable product, but his lack of financial savvy was hurting his business. In other words, he needed a person who was knowledgeable and competent in finances to keep him in check. He also needed a marketing organization that could propel his products to markets beyond his immediate reach. Once there were people to handle the finances and marketing, the company began to thrive. Similarly, the fishermen were passionate about their work, but to achieve success, they had to overcome their reluctance to work together, as well as find other individuals to help market their tuna and control the company's finances. In other words, it seemed to me that the key to success was passion and teamwork.

Since my experience in Esperance, I have been doing three things:

- Teaching entrepreneurs how to start businesses that address the product, marketing, and financial areas of the company equally well.

- Training Enterprise Facilitators to work in communities and help transform the local economies one passionate person at a time.

- Teaching the Trinity of Management model to practitioners.

Every conversation I have with would-be entrepreneurs starts with the question I posed at the beginning of this book: What is your passion? How to Start a Business and Ignite Your Life is inspired by the thousands of answers I have received over the years. It is also based on my research on the most famous and successful entrepreneurs from the past two centuries, which reveals several key features of successful entrepreneurship. One of the most important, though, is this: General Motors, Ford, Carnegie, US Steel, NCR, IBM, Standard Oil, Disney, Yahoo, Kellogg's, Starbucks, Google, JC Penney, 3M, AT&T, Nike, Intel, Apple, McDonald's, Sony, Microsoft, Facebook, and Twitter did not succeed because of the efforts of a single individual. The thing all of these companies have in common is that not one of them was started by one person. At their inception, there were always two, three, or four people. Like Mauri and the fishermen, the founders of these corporations formed teams of talented, passionate individuals. The bottom line is that no one—and I mean no one—can do it all. If you remain alone in business, you will not succeed. This basic understanding is what led me to develop a personality-based management model and coaching technique that I call the Trinity of Management®, which is the heart of this book.

The Trinity of Management, which you will learn about more in Chapter 2 (see page 17), is based on the related concepts of passion and effective teamwork. It recognizes that people have different personalities, abilities, strengths, and talents needed to excel at their respective passions. This model is also based on the principle that one person cannot possibly have all the talent and knowledge required to run a successful business. Finally, it supports my belief that successful entrepreneurs do only what they love to do in their businesses, but surround themselves with capable people who love to do the rest.

While this may seem like logical advice, the Trinity of Management has been met with resistance by many of my clients over the years. I have been asked questions such as, "How can I form a team if I don't have enough money to pay even myself?" and have heard excuses like, "I don't trust anybody with my business;" "I need money, not advice;" and "I can't find anyone worth employing." Such resistance is one major reason why I felt compelled to write this book—to help entrepreneurs understand that they cannot achieve success when they try to run their businesses alone. The death of the entrepreneur is solitude.

I also wrote this book as a counterargument to a common misconception in our culture, namely, that entrepreneurs should be able to "do it all." You yourself may have been told that you should know everything there is to know about business, and you have probably read about famous entrepreneurs who are portrayed as heroes and geniuses. But the truth is that many of these hugely successful entrepreneurs did not know everything about business; in fact, most of them never even studied business! They brought in others to help them run their companies. I always smile at the story of how Henry Ford got so mad at his accounting department that he threw all their office furniture out of the first-floor window!

Last but not least, I wrote this book because I have witnessed first-hand the success of the Trinity of Management and its power to transform businesses, as well as people's lives. For more than three decades, I have been teaching this model, and the businesses that practice these principles have an extraordinary sustainability level—more than 80 percent of them remain open after five years. This statistic alone made me realize that it was time to take the Trinity of Management to a wider audience. You are now holding the result of many years' worth of hard work, research, and success in your hands. I sincerely hope that you wisely invest the time needed to figure out who you are as an entrepreneur, because only then can you go about finding the right people to help you. Although it takes a team to succeed, you are where your business begins.

Introduction

What makes an entrepreneur successful? Some may argue that it takes genius and vision, or a ground-breaking product or service. Others may say education and years of training. And still others may insist that it all comes down to money and publicity. Certainly, all of these things are helpful and can contribute to the success of a business, but not a single one alone determines whether or not an entrepreneur's risk ultimately pays off. So what does? This is the question that you must ask yourself when starting your own business, and the one that this book both explores and answers.

I have counseled aspiring and struggling entrepreneurs for three decades, and if my work has taught me anything, it's that personality plays an intricate—and often overlooked—role in business. Our personalities shape our interests, skills, and talents; they determine our strengths and weaknesses; and they make us better suited to certain professions. This understanding is crucial for entrepreneurs, who all too often try to singlehandedly run a business that, by its very nature, is multifaceted and requires a wide range of skills. For starters, every business must have someone to make a product or provide a service, someone to market and sell the product to the public, and someone to oversee finances and make sure bills are paid on time. Obviously, these tasks are very different and, therefore, more closely matched to certain personality types than others. One individual cannot possibly excel in all of these areas. More importantly, no one, not even the most ingenious entrepreneur, is passionate about every area of a business. And ultimately, it is passion that sustains companies.

The relationship between business, personality, and passion lies at the heart of the Trinity of Management, a business model and philosophy that I believe should guide every entrepreneur. This model recognizes that a business is the sum of its individual parts, and in order for the business to succeed, every part must be managed by a person who is adept, motivated, and passionate. In other words, the success of a business is dependent not only on the ideas and expertise of the entrepreneur, but also the talents of others. The most fundamental principle of the Trinity of Management is this: Entrepreneurs should focus on the area of business that they love, and surround themselves with people who love the other areas. This simple piece of wisdom is the foundation of nearly every successful enterprise.

The Trinity of Management is one of the central tenets of *How to Start a Business and Ignite Your Life*. This book has been designed to guide you through the process of starting your own business, from selecting the area of business for which you are best suited, to forming your team, to writing a business plan, and everything in between. If you already have your own business, this book will answer many questions you may have or shed light on problems that your company is currently facing. It also challenges the common perception that entrepreneurs are geniuses who can "do it all" in business, and reveals how this myth only hurts business owners.

Chapter 1 explores the question of what makes a business successful, explaining the roles that psychology, personality, and passion play in shaping entrepreneurs. Then, Chapter 2 takes a more in-depth look at the Trinity of Management business model and provides overviews of the three most significant areas of any business—product, marketing, and financial management. Chapters 3, 4, and 5 cover the three areas in greater detail and describe the type of personality best suited to each role in the Trinity. In these chapters, I also present examples of "good" and "bad" product people, marketers, and financial managers, accompanied by stories of success and failure. This information will help you understand the strengths that allow them to thrive in their positions, as well as the weaknesses that can cause their downfall. At the end of each of these chapters is a questionnaire that has been created to help you select which area of business is the right one for your personality. If you already own a company, the self-assessments will allow you to reflect on whether you are currently focusing on the area in which you excel, or stuck doing work that you find difficult or uninspiring.

The last chapters of this book contain important practical advice for running a business using the Trinity of Management model. This guidance, which covers topics such as choosing business team members and seeking financial assistance, is based on what I have learned as an Enterprise Facilitator over the past three decades. I also expose several common misconceptions about business and tell you how to objectively assess the quality of your company's (present or future) management. This information is vital to ensure that your business stays viable or, alternatively, to restore the health of your ailing company.

One thing I must make absolutely clear, though, is that this book is intended for people who are truly passionate and want to turn their passion into successful business ventures. If you are hoping to start your own business simply to make money, you should close this book right now. Entrepreneurs whose sole motivation is money will not have long-term success. Rather, it is passion that drives successful entrepreneurs, and allows them to surmount the trials and tribulations involved in entrepreneurship.

By the time you have read this book, you will understand that you cannot fulfill your dreams unless you have two basic things: passion and a passionate team. You will also understand the significance of the quote, "On our own, we are like an exquisite high speed aircraft which, for lack of a tiny part, is left stranded beside the runway, rendered slower than a tractor or bicycle."[1] Yes, it is possible for you to make your ideas and dreams a reality and turn your passion into a sustainable living. But the key to this transformation is the Trinity of Management. So read on and be empowered to start a business, vitalize your company, and ignite your life.

1

Why Some Entrepreneurs Succeed While Others Fail

When it comes to managing a business, why do some people with remarkable skill, knowledge, work ethic, and integrity fail, while others succeed seemingly without effort? What makes these people successful? Is there a "secret" to making it in business? Does success require natural talent and innate business acumen? Or does it ultimately come down to luck?

This chapter provides a foundation for answering these core questions by examining some commonalities among business owners whom I have observed over the years. Based on your own experiences, you may recognize many of these characteristics. They can—and often do—make the difference between success and failure.

MY INTRODUCTION TO ENTREPRENEURSHIP

My experience with entrepreneurship dates back to my childhood, when my father attempted to start his own medical practice. Descending from a long line of doctors and pharmacists, my father loved medicine and devoted his life to the profession. He graduated at the top of his medical school class, specialized in radiology, and went into private practice in his hometown, a small village in Italy. The practice was successful—my father was a skilled, dedicated physician, and his family's reputation garnered a loyal clientele. And since he was one of only three doctors in the community, competition was minimal.

Eventually, my father decided to move his entire practice to Rome, believing the city's large population would surely mean more patients and a better living. He knew he would be unknown at first but thought that his expansive knowledge, quality care, and professionalism would be enough to attract clients. It seemed like the perfect decision.

Yet, the reality did not match my father's expectations. In Rome, he was one of thousands of doctors who had established practices in the suburbs built after World War II. His last name was not the effective marketing strategy it had been in his hometown, and self-promotion was unthinkable for my quiet, reserved father. He wouldn't even introduce himself to the local pharmacist, who had a booming business only half a block away! As a result, the practice did poorly.

My father subsidized his practice by selling real estate on the side, but even this extra source of income was insufficient to cover all the expenses. He was finally forced to give up his dream and work for a foreign government-run hospital. Although the new job alleviated our anxiety and unhappiness, my father's disappointing encounter with entrepreneurship was not forgotten in our family. The experience shaped my childhood and left me mystified about business, as well as what it takes to make one successful.

This question lingered even into the first few years of my career working with entrepreneurs. In the mid-1980s, I had begun working with a group of people who, like me, believed that entrepreneurs could fulfill their goals and dreams if only they had someone to guide and advise them. We devised a novel method of helping entrepreneurs that we named Enterprise Facilitation, and formed a company, Entrepreneur Facilitation, to assist them in creating and managing successful businesses. I met many talented individuals who, for various reasons, struggled to maintain their businesses. One person who stands out in my mind is Mauri, my first client. Mauri could produce delicious smoked fish, but lacked marketing and money-management skills. He possessed the passion and skill to make a great product, but needed help turning his talents into lucrative work.

This was the case for many other craftspeople with whom I worked. They were extremely proficient in their particular skill yet deficient in other areas, like marketing and finance. Some were too shy to promote and sell their goods. Some missed appointments with potential retailers or were reluctant to bring their products to the market, relentlessly fine-tuning and reworking them instead. Others did not understand finances and made poor pricing decisions by, for example, discounting their products below manufacturing costs.

At the same time, I met people with brilliant marketing skills but without a reliable product to sell. I encountered people with a strong grasp of numbers and money, but without a business to financially manage. Others I met were "serial entrepreneurs"—individuals with a string of failed businesses to their name. They would start a business only to go broke in a year or two and then promptly move on to the next venture, confident that this would be the one to "hit it big." I also encountered several poor, frustrated farmers who acknowledged that they needed to make more money but were terrified about the risks involved in changing their traditional ways of doing business. In sum, my work involved an endless procession of people who, for numerous reasons, could neither get their new businesses off the ground nor improve their existing ones.

Back then, I still subscribed to the belief that entrepreneurs had to learn how to "do it all" in their business, from producing the service or product to selling it and, above all, managing the money. The idea that entrepreneurs need to be skillful in all aspects of business was— and still is—a theory that is commonly taught and believed, so who was I to disagree? Yet, I was now being confronted on a daily basis by clients who could not manage every facet of their business. Consequently, I began to question this popular theory of successful entrepreneurship. I urged my clients to seek help in the areas in which they were ineffective or lacked knowledge: "If you cannot do it, if you will not do it, or if you hate doing it," I told them, "then find someone who can do it for you."

THE MYTH OF THE "PERFECT" ENTREPRENEUR

Many clients agreed with my advice. Others resisted the idea of having other people run the parts of their businesses that they were mismanaging or neglecting outright. I realized it was because they felt inadequate and even guilty that they were unable to "do it all" well. But instead of trying to fix the problem, they made excuses. Some common ones included:

- "The product is so good that it will sell itself as soon as it's discovered."

- "I'm not going to pay some fast talker to sell my service. Nobody knows what I do better than me, so I'm the best person to sell it—I just don't have the time."

- "Why should I trust someone else with my money?"

- "I don't have the money yet to pay for someone else to help me."

My clients never assumed responsibility for their ailing businesses. Instead, they blamed the banks, their lack of money, the government, or the weather; it was never their fault when the businesses failed. They were defensive and defiant, and it took me some time to figure out why they were so reluctant to get help. I eventually realized that these business owners were insistent on "doing it all" because of a myth that is both engrained in our culture and promoted by the media. It is the myth of the rugged, self-reliant entrepreneur who knows it all and can do it all—the myth of the perfect entrepreneur.

After a presentation I gave many years ago, a young woman came over to me and said, "You know, you are the only person I have ever heard that advises people against trying to run a business alone. My first business went bankrupt ten years ago, and it took me seven years to recover, both economically and psychologically. Three years ago, I started a new business, and I'm already going broke again!" She continued, "My problem is that I'm not good at managing money. But when my sister, an accountant, offered to do the bookkeeping, I told her that as a businesswoman, I have to learn how to do everything myself." When I asked her why, she insisted that businesspeople should be knowledgeable and capable of running all aspects of a business. Maybe this is what she was taught in business school, but another possibility is that she had bought into the media-driven myth of the perfect, know-it-all entrepreneur.

The media has long loved a hero. From the time we are children, we read about heroes both real and fictional. We idolize superheroes like Superman who can really do it all—fly, repel bullets, carry trucks and buses, and leap over tall buildings. (Although, come to think of it, we never saw him try to run a business—but that's another point entirely.) We hear about people from all walks of life who are considered "superheroes" in their fields. This is certainly true for the pioneers of the business world, from Henry Ford and Walt Disney to the young entrepreneurs who launched the first dot-com companies in the 1990s when they were barely out of high school. These are the entrepreneurs seen on TV, plastered on the glossy covers of business magazines, and touted by the media as the "Top 10 Entrepreneurs of the Year." They are portrayed as visionaries and geniuses who possess special gifts and a unique kind of courage.

In other words, according to the popular image created and lionized by the media, entrepreneurs are an exceptional breed of individuals who know it all and can do it all; they are super-humans, not ordinary people. And this misrepresentation was the basis of my clients' knowledge of entrepreneurship. They had never heard stories about entrepreneurs who were like them: Regular people with skills, courage, ambition, and the willingness to put everything on the line in pursuit of a dream, but who did not and could not take care of every aspect of business. I rejected the idea that you had to somehow magically transform from Clark Kent into Superman in order to be a successful entrepreneur. This myth was only leaving my clients and other would-be business owners frustrated, hopeless, and destitute. I believed that if they accepted the fact they were not Superman and then accepted help from others, their businesses could thrive.

THE BUSINESS OF LEARNING ABOUT BUSINESS

Although my clients needed guidance, business school was not necessarily the answer to their problems. Business school is widely considered to be the key to "making it" in business, but it's important to keep in mind two principal facts:

1. There are entrepreneurs who have launched successful companies and made millions, even billions, of dollars without having ever attended business school. For example, consider the entrepreneurs of the 1920s, 30s, and 40s who started companies in parts of the world where business school was still nonexistent. Many of the greatest entrepreneurs of all time never took a single course in the subject.

2. There are people who have gone to business school and then started businesses that ultimately went broke. In fact, statistics show that people who have a business school education fail in business just as frequently as those who do not.

Of course, there are many positive sides to business school. Business is an interesting, dynamic field that is worth learning, and there are plenty of courses that can provide a solid foundation in the nuts and bolts of running a business. Still, judging from the facts above, business school will probably not make you an expert in an area of business in which you are not comfortable. Business courses can give you basic knowledge, which is valuable for any aspiring entrepreneur, but they do not guarantee that you will be able to handle every aspect of your business. Simply put, not everyone is cut out for *every* area—and that is perfectly fine. The fields in which you excel are ultimately determined by your individual skills, interests, and talents, which are themselves influenced by your personality and psychological makeup.

PSYCHOLOGY, PERSONALITY, AND BUSINESS

As I worked towards building a successful business model for my clients, I began to ask myself if we are suited to certain hobbies, activities, and professions based on our psychological makeup and individual personalities. Perhaps, I wondered, we succeed only in those areas that come naturally to us and that we enjoy, and, maybe we only enjoy what comes naturally to us. If this is the case, then the reverse must also be true—namely, that we do not excel at things for which we are not psychologically suited and that hold little interest or enjoyment for us. People who are athletic, for example, tend to love sports and excel in the sport of their choice. On the other hand, those who are not athletically inclined most likely do not enjoy sports, nor do they become professional athletes. It seems logical to me that this correlation would also apply to business interests.

Although it has not yet been conclusively proven, research has shown that a significant part of human beings' psychological makeup is inherited. Studies have also found a link between brain function and personality. At some point in the future, scientists may be able to confirm that the human brain is hardwired and that personalities are not changeable. In other words, science may reveal that how people perceive the world is an innate characteristic.[1] This is a controversial topic among psychologists, many of whom maintain that upbringing and other environmental factors determine personality. This position, though, does not account for the clear differences in personality among babies—even twins!

One psychologist's theory of personality is particularly relevant to the study of entrepreneurs and success in business. In addition to other important theories of personality (see the inset on page 12), Carl Jung famously identified two main personality types, *introverts* and *extroverts*. According to Jung, introverts experience the world inwardly through perceptions, thoughts, dreams, and emotions, and tend to be less engaged with the external environment. In contrast, extroverts are gregarious and assertive, and external factors drive their thoughts, feelings, and dreams rather than the other way around.

Isabel Myers and Katharine Briggs, two well-known students of Jung, applied this theory of extroversion and introversion to the professional world. They said that introverts are more commonly found in areas such as medicine and the sciences, while extroverts dominate in fields like marketing, public relations, sales, and communications. This should come as no surprise; after all, doctors, accountants, and scientists, for example, are often engaged in independent work and focused on deepening their knowledge of their field, while professions in marketing and sales involve direct interaction with others.

It seems that what may prevent people from excelling in certain occupations is not a matter of intellect but psychological makeup. The problem for my father—who graduated summa cum laude from medical school—was clearly not a lack of intelligence. His medical practice failed because it was not marketed properly, since he did not have an aptitude for marketing or a desire to learn it. In fact, he despised marketing so much that he ultimately chose to give up his practice rather than figure out how to promote it.

More About Personality

There are many theories about the psychological dimensions of the human personality. For instance, in addition to extroversion and introversion, Carl Jung identified four basic ways that human beings interact with the world:

1. **Thinking.** This refers to intellectual cognition as a way of evaluating information or ideas rationally and logically. Jung called thinking a *rational function*, meaning that it involves decision-making or judgment rather than the simple intake of information.

2. **Feeling.** Like thinking, feeling is a matter of evaluating information, but one that involves weighing your emotional—not logical—response. Jung also described this function as rational, but obviously not in the usual sense of the word.

3. **Sensation.** This means that you acquire information by way of the senses and, therefore, are skilled at listening and making good observations. Jung referred to sensation as an *irrational function*, since it involves perceiving information rather than judging it.

4. **Intuition.** A type of perception that works outside of the usual conscious processes, intuition can be likened to "seeing around corners." It is irrational (perceptual) like sensation, but entails the complex integration of large amounts of information rather than simple seeing or hearing.

To summarize, psychology and personality, which are closely interconnected, help explain why people are exceptional in certain areas and not others. In addition, they explain how skills and interests are developed, as well as how these skills and interests affect career choices. Asking people, including my clients, to become adept in areas completely contrary to their talents, skills, and areas of intelligence is like asking an accountant to become a professional dancer or fisherman. At best, it is possible to become merely adequate in an area that presents difficulty. Unfortunately, there is no place for mediocrity in small businesses, where the margin of error is also small. Large

Another landmark study on personality was published by Paul Costa and Robert McCrae in 1992. Their findings distinguished five main personality dimensions and their associated characteristics, as seen in the table below.

PERSONALITY DIMENSIONS AND THE POLES OF TRAITS THEY FORM (COSTA AND MCCRAE, 1992)		
PERSONALITY DIMENSION	**HIGH-LEVEL TRAITS**	**LOW-LEVEL TRAITS**
Neuroticism	Sensitive, nervous	Secure, confident
Extraversion	Outgoing, energetic	Shy, withdrawn
Openness to experience	Inventive, curious	Cautious, conservative
Agreeableness	Friendly, compassionate	Competitive, outspoken
Conscientiousness	Efficient, organized	Easygoing, careless

Theories of human personality like those above can be used to explain why people choose certain career paths over others. It makes sense that someone who is very quiet and thoughtful would prefer a different line of work than a person who prefers to engage with others. Similarly, a profession such as teaching is better suited to an individual who is friendly and compassionate rather than nervous and withdrawn. Working in an occupation that is contrary to your personality may result in a high level of dissatisfaction and affect your level of success.

corporations can withstand mistakes and mediocrity, but a blunder in a smaller company can be extremely costly. In order for a small business to succeed, each person must excel in his or her role, and doing so requires passion.

PASSION—A KEY TO SUCCESS

If money was the primary motivator, everyone would pursue only the highest-paying occupations. Obviously, this is not the case, as there are millions of people in all corners of the world working in a wide range of professions and establishing all sorts of businesses. It seems that the path many people take in life is based not on money, but rather on personal interests and abilities.

The tendency to pursue what we enjoy, as well as excel at it, is usually evident at a young age. In my case, this is true. I lived overseas for three years and, during that time, attended a private school that placed a high value on creativity, leadership, languages, and sports. I enjoyed learning Arabic, English, and Italian; I developed an interest in soccer; I even liked helping to repaint the school with my classmates and teachers just for fun. My Italian literature instructor praised my essays, which she described as "so free and so creative," and asked my parents if she could keep them. I even received a gold medal for academic achievement. Yet, it seemed to me that I had not done anything special to deserve it—I was simply being myself, having fun, and, at the same time, excelling at subjects that I loved.

When I was eleven, my family moved back to Italy and my parents enrolled me in a public school in Rome. There were stark differences between this new school and the foreign private school I had loved. Here, the class sizes were large and the curriculum focused on algebra, calculus, composition, and grammar—none of which were my strong suits. In fact, my Italian teacher called my parents at the end of the school year and recommended that they start looking for a special school that could better fulfill my "special needs." This should give you an idea of how I fared academically that year. According to the Italian teacher, I earned the lowest average in the school's recorded history. So, in just one year, I went from being a gold medal student to the so-called "class dunce." How was this possible? It's unlikely that my IQ would have decreased so dramatically. A better explanation is that I was not learning about things that excited me, so I was not excelling academically.

Think about your years in school. What subjects were enjoyable for you and which ones did you find boring? Did you do well in the subjects you enjoyed? Did they come naturally to you? Does your current occupation reflect the classes you loved? On the other hand, do you remember anything you learned in the classes you despised?

Like favorite school subjects and activities, we choose careers based on who we are—our personalities, our interests, and above all, our passions. To become a successful entrepreneur, which requires a substantial investment of time and effort, you must be passionate about your work. Although you can learn the basic principles and "how-to's," you will never excel in a specific area of business if you are not passionate about it. There is a huge difference between being able to do something and having a passion for doing something. People who have passion—a word derived from the Latin word meaning "to suffer"—are so in love with their chosen field that they are prepared to do whatever it takes to achieve their goal. They remain focused, sometimes for years, on mastering their art, craft, skill, or profession. Plain and simple, passion is a key to success, but it is not all that is required.

CONCLUSION

So, to return to the question that opened this chapter, why do some entrepreneurs succeed while others fail? It is obvious that not every successful businessperson is the "perfect" entrepreneur so often mythologized by the media. Additionally, most entrepreneurs' success stories do not involve A's in business courses or even a business school education.

Success is based on individuals. It is about the introvert developing a passion for something that he or she discovers within themselves and wants to explore. It is about the extrovert embracing the external world, reaching out to others, and asking them to hear what he or she has to say. Based on our psychological makeup and personality traits, we develop a passion for something that we do well. It is this passion that leads many people into business; it is this same passion that determines success or failure.

The successful entrepreneurs I have observed, read about, and advised have one thing in common: They recognize that their passion alone will not make them successful. They get help. Simply put, successful entrepreneurs do only what they love to do in the company, and they find talented people who love to do the rest.

Years after his failed first attempt at a establishing a medical practice in Rome, my father met a man who was a true extrovert and passionate about marketing. They joined forces, and my father and his partner started their own private practice. They were incredibly successful.

Achieving success in business is a matter of bringing together a group of highly motivated people who possess both passion and skill in the three major areas of business: doing, selling, and financially managing. The next chapter takes a closer look at these three areas that comprise a successful business, which are known collectively as the Trinity of Management.

2

The Trinity of Management

Forget about the myth of the "perfect" entrepreneur. Forget about trying to learn it all, know it all, and do it all. Goodbye and good riddance. The real everyday entrepreneur who has succeeded in business will tell you that it is the effort of a *team*—not a single individual—that enables an enterprise to prosper and grow. This team is the Trinity of Management, a business model that encompasses the key components every company needs in order to be successful. The Trinity of Management model, though basic, has been used by the most successful entrepreneurs. It is based on the idea that businesses have three main areas: product or service development, marketing, and financial management. This chapter introduces you to these three areas and examines the personality type that can best fulfill each role. But first I will explain why a cohesive, passionate team can achieve far more in a business than an individual, no matter how brilliant she may be.

MICHAEL JORDAN AND THE "TRIANGLE OFFENSE"

The Trinity of Management relies on both individual excellence and effective teamwork. In order for the Trinity to operate efficiently, the team members must combine their personal talents to achieve the best possible outcome. This dynamic is often seen in sports and is perhaps best exemplified by the relationship between Michael Jordan and Phil Jackson, the Chicago Bulls' head coach during the peak of

17

Jordan's career. Many people assume that Michael Jordan was the sole driving force behind the six championships the Bulls won over eight years, but this is not the case. It was actually Michael Jordan's unrivaled talent in combination with Phil Jackson's brilliant team strategy—the famous "Triangle Offense"—that ultimately earned the Bulls their titles.

Let's start at the beginning. From a young age, Michael Jordan was passionate about basketball and worked tirelessly at honing his skill. He was quickly recognized by his peers as a true talent and a force to be reckoned with. But in the NBA, the competition was tough, and Jordan became the focus of opposing teams' defensive strategies. The goal was to stop Jordan at all costs and prevent him from scoring. As the former Detroit Pistons' coach, Chuck Daly, explains, "If Michael was at the point, we forced him left and [double-teamed] him. If he was on the left wing, we went immediately to a double team from the top. . . . The other rule was, any time [Jordan] went by you, you had to nail him. If he was coming off a screen, nail him. We didn't want to be dirty—I know some people thought we were—but we had to make contact and be very physical."[1] These so-called "Jordan Rules" effectively stopped the Bulls from winning the championship two years in a row, thereby demonstrating the power of the team over the individual.

It was Phil Jackson's leadership that turned the tide in favor of the Bulls. Jackson implemented the "Triangle Offense," a strategy in which the team's most brilliant player (in this case, Michael Jordan) relinquishes the ball instead of controlling it. Every player on the court has an assigned role. This approach not only made Michael Jordan less of a target for the opposing team, but also enhanced the performance of every team member. Sports analysts have long agreed that the Bulls improved as a team when each individual player took on responsibility instead of it all resting on Jordan: "Jordan had already established himself as an elite NBA superstar by single-handedly turning Chicago into a playoff contender. However, by sharing responsibility rather than shouldering it, he continued to blossom as a great all-around basketball player. More importantly, the Bulls also improved notably as a team."[2]

Phil Jackson's Triangle Offense strategy strongly parallels the Trinity of Management model and serves as an apt example for aspiring entrepreneurs. You may be passionate, talented, and a "master" in your particular field, but it takes more than these traits to make your business thrive. Success lies in the sum of the parts—the team. The Trinity of Management is about "sharing the ball" in order to achieve victory.

THE COMPONENTS OF THE TRINITY OF MANAGEMENT

Like basketball players, every single member of a business team should have a distinct role with specific responsibilities. First, there should be a product person, or "doer," who makes the product or provides the service sold by the business. Second, there needs to be a marketer, who spreads the word about the product or service, and focuses on making sales. And finally, there must be a financial manager to handle all money matters and make sure the business is making a profit.

Clearly, these roles require different skills and are better suited to certain people based on individual personalities, interests, and strengths. In order for the Trinity of Management to work, though, you first need to figure out into which category *you* fall. In other words, you need to know who you are before you can put together a strong team. As explained in Chapter 1, the idea that entrepreneurs should be able to "do it all" in a company is a complete fallacy and only hurts businesses in the long run. Like Michael Jordan, you need to be able to "pass the ball" to others who are more adept in certain areas. Sharing responsibility and playing to each other's strengths ultimately puts more points on the scoreboard for your business.

So now the question is: What type of business person are you? When I pose this question to clients, I use the diagram depicted on page 20 to clearly illustrate the Trinity of Management.

Imagine that the smiling face is you, the entrepreneur at the top of the company. The three boxes represent the three areas of the Trinity of Management—products (P), marketing (M), and financial management (FM). You may already know the category into which you fall,

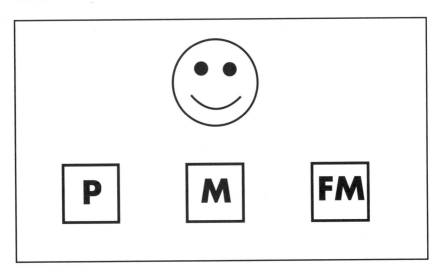

Trinity of Management

but if you are like other entrepreneurs with whom I have worked, you may be so used to juggling tasks that you have lost sight of your true passion. And before you can form a business team and implement the Trinity of Management model, you must know who *you* are. As an entrepreneur, you must identify your passion, recognize your talents, and focus on cultivating skills that come naturally to you. Let's begin this self-assessment by exploring the basic functions and characteristics of each role in the Trinity.

Are You a Product Person?

The product people are a company's "doers"—the ones who deliver a product or service to consumers. A product person can create an invention, design or manufacture goods, or offer some kind of service, such as medical care or plumbing. Product people of a business are also those who oversee the creation and distribution of goods or services, like chief operating officers (COOs).

True product people are what I call "lovers"—individuals who have discovered their passion and are committed to pursuing it. Lovers are the opposite of "tourists," which is the term I use to describe those who continuously move from one occupation to another in search of something that motivates and excites them. "Tourists" are not effective product people due to their lack of clarity, focus, and passion. "Lovers," though, take great pride in their work and truly believe that the product or service they provide is unique and valuable. They also strive for excellence and are not satisfied until they meet the high standards they set for themselves.

Are You a Marketer?

Even the most useful, impressive, and innovative product will remain unsold if no one knows it is available. The primary function and goal of the marketer is to make products and services visible by bringing them to the marketplace, which can be local or global in Marketing people are effective communicators and highly skilled when it comes to the dissemination of information, which today is increasingly driven by the internet, social media, and high-tech mobile devices. Marketers are also passionate about connecting with consumers and generating sales. The best marketers are the ones who truly believe in the product they sell, since this makes them more committed to spreading the word about it. The most effective marketers are extroverted, curious, and in touch with the needs of the intended market.

Are You a Financial Manager?

More than just figures and numbers, financial management requires an understanding of the true cost of maintaining a business. Focusing on the "bottom line," financial managers do not simply act as bookkeepers but enable businesses to stay above ground. They help the CEO (or CEO-equivalent) of a company make responsible financial decisions, as well as ensure that monetary resources are used sensibly. The best financial managers clearly understand the economic climate and its impact on business, and take great satisfaction in seeing a business prosper.

Hopefully, these brief descriptions have given you a better idea of the kind of entrepreneur you are or, at least, the kind you are not. Recognizing traits that do *not* apply to you is just as important when it comes to forming your team. After all, the Trinity of Management operates best when every person is both skilled in and passionate about her area. As an entrepreneur, you must exude passion, and this is possible only when you have a strong sense of who you are. Now the key is to find your business's missing pieces—your "teammates."

FORMING YOUR TEAM

It's important to note that applying the word "management" to the Trinity of Management is slightly inaccurate and misleading; however, there is no better alternative. Derived from the French language, *management* literally means to physically handle animals, particularly horses, and suggests a forceful action. But for most businesses, there is no real management in the beginning. This is because at the inception of a company, there needs to be a group of talented individuals who want to work together and can operate as a selfless team. Management comes into play later on when harmony and cooperation must be maintained. Forming a business team does not take managerial skills, but rather an eye for passion, dedication, and talent.

As explained in Chapter 1, the key positions in a business must be held by talented individuals who are adept in and suited to those positions. Similar to the literal meaning of passion (to suffer), "talent" comes from the Greek word meaning "to endure or to bear." Passion and talent are closely intertwined. Passionate people endure the hardship involved in honing a talent, and they continue the struggle even without the guarantee of financial gain. It is this level of dedication that puts them at the top of their game and, in turn, makes them an asset to a business. And in order to attract this type of dedicated, passionate person to your business team, you need to exhibit passion and commitment as well.

CONCLUSION

The Trinity of Management is a business model and philosophy rooted in the idea that a team can accomplish more together than an individual can alone. Still, in order for the Trinity to work, talented, capable individuals must fill the key positions—product development, marketing, and financial management. Like Phil Jackson's "Triangle Offense," the Trinity of Management is a combination of teamwork and individual passion, talent, and skill. The upcoming chapters cover the three components of the Trinity of Management in more detail so that you can better assess your team, as well as yourself, as you begin your business venture.

3

The "Ps" of Business— Product People

"You can't just ask customers what they want and then try to give that to them. By the time you get it built, they'll want something new."

—STEVE JOBS

Take a moment to look around you. Everything you see is the result of someone's innovative thinking: the chair in which you're sitting, the computer in front of you, the software program you're using, the lighting above you, and the cars, trucks, and buses driving past your window. All of these things, which started as the ideas of passionate, talented individuals, are *products*—things that are designed, developed, built or manufactured, and made available to a market. Products, which can be physical objects or services, range from hamburgers to data-processing operations and from hats to massages. The person who creates the product or delivers the service— and genuinely loves doing so—is who I call the product person, or "P," of a business.

The impact of product people is significant and far-reaching. Not only have they literally engineered, assembled, and wired the world that you inhabit, but they have also delivered you into the world, taught you how to read, provided you with clothes and housing, and introduced you to music, technology, and good food. Product people include artists, craftspeople, inventors, engineers, technicians, actors, hairdressers, chefs, dancers, farmers, and journalists. Teachers, doctors, bakers, butchers, and plumbers, as well as manual workers, foremen, and chief operating officers (COOs) are also considered product people. Simply put, a world without product people is inconceivable. They are the "doers" whose sweat and tears facilitate creation and innovation.

Although passion is what drives the success of product people, it can also be their downfall. If left unchecked, some product people may become delusional and blinded by the love they have for their work. This chapter introduces you to "good" and "bad" product people. Being able to identify the positive and negative traits of a product person will help you form a strong business team and increase your chances of success.

GOOD PRODUCT PEOPLE

As mentioned in Chapter 2, I believe there are two kinds of people in this world—tourists and lovers. Tourists are people who move from one career to another in search of a passion to motivate and inspire them. Lovers, on the other hand, are people who have already found their passion and are committed to cultivating it, regardless of how long or hard the struggle. True product people are lovers; they fully enjoy and are completely absorbed by their chosen field. They believe that their product or service is unique and important, and they are determined to perfect it.

Yet, there is more to a *good* product person than passion and talent. Good product people understand that success in business does not rest solely on a great product, but requires effective marketing and smart financial decision-making in addition to the great product or service. Willing to recognize their weaknesses, good product people trust others to sell their product and handle the finances. As a result, the product person can focus on whatever it is that he does best, whether designing, drawing, painting, cooking, building, teaching, or repairing. The inventor can return to his workspace, the artist can continue to paint, and the scientist can spend more time in the lab refining his product and exploring its possibilities. In these particular situations, innovation thrives.

Consider Henry Ford as an example. He didn't stop at the Model T but went on to develop better models. Furthermore, he did not wait to find out what consumers wanted before he invented the affordable car. "If I [had] asked people what they wanted, they would have said a faster horse," Ford once quipped. Like Henry Ford, good product people strive to stay one step ahead of the market by constantly improving and evolving their product. If consumers like Disneyland, you give them Disney World. If they like the iPhone, you give them the iPad. Innovation comes about when product people have the opportunity to concentrate on their passion, as others work on selling it and paying the bills.

It's important to point out that many companies do not have a single product person. Sometimes, two or more talented product people team up to create a valuable product and start a business. The product people behind Google, Larry Page and Sergey Brin, were PhD students at Stanford University in California when they embarked on their quest to build a better search engine. Page and Brin studied the search engines that were currently available and were determined to design one that was superior. The product that ultimately resulted from their efforts, Google, was not a completely original concept, but it met an existing need much more efficiently. The rest is history.

Yet, not all product people realize that they have a great product. In some cases, marketers or financial managers may take notice of a product person's talent and help him harness his abilities so that he can become a part of an entrepreneurial team. A marketer might ask a local craftsperson, "Did you ever think of selling your craft all over the world?" This simple question can be the beginning of a lucrative business venture. Likewise, a financial manager may offer to keep track of profits, expenses, and other money-related issues if an inventor agrees to increase production of his new gadget. This, too, is an example of maximizing the potential of a good product person.

In sum, good product people are passionate about whatever it is they create or provide, whether a new fishing apparatus or an online dating service. They want to offer the best product or service possible, and they are unwavering in their effort to do so. At the same time, good product people are aware that they will not succeed if they work in isolation, and they are comfortable allowing others to handle important tasks that they themselves are not good at. In a successful business, good product people truly appreciate and trust their team, which allows them to focus on what they do best—creating the best product or service that they can.

BAD PRODUCT PEOPLE

Good product people, though passionate, have realistic expectations and understand the importance of a well-rounded business team. By contrast, bad product people believe that if they offer a product or service that is better than what is currently on the market, the world will beat a path to their door. They are so passionate about their work that they simply cannot fathom how anyone could fail to see how unique, valuable, and important their products or services are. Consequently, they are usually bitter when the world does *not* show up at their door—which probably doesn't have a sign on it advertising, "Better Product Found Here."

It's likely that you are already familiar with bad product people. They are the artists who shut themselves away in their studios and never show their paintings to others. They are the scientists and inventors holed up in their labs with brilliant creations that they refuse to take to the market. They are the technical geniuses who show up to meetings with venture capitalists holding 600 pages of incomprehensible jargon and complain that nobody understands them. Some bad product people are arrogant, believing that no one else is worthy of seeing their work. Others are temperamental and respond unfavorably to any kind of criticism. In other cases, they want other people to enjoy their product or service, but are convinced that marketing is unnecessary because their product is *that* great. They often do not realize that insisting upon their product's greatness can come across as insecurity or insincerity, thereby turning off potential customers. After all, it is the market that ultimately decides whether or not a

Steve Jobs—A Product Person's Success Story

Steve Jobs exemplifies the passionate product person like few others of our generation. Although he has been described as an obsessive perfectionist by many who worked for him, Jobs' perfectionism, commitment, and passion—defining qualities of a product person—also drove his success as an entrepreneur. Not only are the Apple products he created technologically groundbreaking, but they are also impeccable in appearance. Jobs made sure that every product, from the iPod to the iPad, had a sophisticated design. In a world of cheaply made electronic goods, he insisted on Apple products being made with Gorilla Glass, a high-quality, damage-resistant material. He also had specialized state-of-the-art factories built all over the world to ensure that Apple's standards were met.

Steve Jobs was an unbending master who settled for nothing but the best when it came to his innovative creations. Because he worked with a team, Jobs was able to focus all of his energy on developing and refining his products and, as a result, he made Apple the multinational corporation that it is today. Through his passion and dedication, Steve Jobs reinvented our culture, giving us both beauty and function in a single portable package. His products, which continue to stun the masses, have made him an icon of our generation and generations to come.

product is "good." Some bad product people avoid taking their product to the market precisely because they do not want to subject it to this final test.

Of course, many bad product people are good, honest people in their everyday lives. They are simply bad businesspeople; their passion blinds them to the fact that even the most ingenious product is useless if no one knows that it exists. You may have heard the commonly asked philosophical question, "If a tree falls in a forest and nobody is around to hear it, does it make a sound?" A similar question can be asked in business as well: If an amazing new device chops down a tree in a matter of seconds but is never marketed to the public, will it sell thousands of units? Of course, the answer is no. My father is an example of this kind of bad "P." His first attempt at starting his own medical practice in Rome, which you read about in Chapter 1, was a failure because instead of finding someone to help him with marketing, he spent all of his money on adding services for a nonexistent clientele. He focused too much on developing his service, and too little on trying to promote it and attract more clients.

This point brings me to another common characteristic of bad product people: They tend to wear financial blinders. While they may acknowledge the need for financial resources, they believe money should be used only for improving the product, with the goal of making it even more irresistible to buyers. This logic overlooks the fact that a business will go broke if all of its money is put back into the product instead of promoting it and helping it sell. Confronted by finances and a market they do not understand, bad product people become fixated on perfecting their product, however unnecessary, simply because it's all they know.

In short, a bad product person is his own worst enemy. And when this type of person is in charge, it's unlikely that the business will succeed. (See the inset on page 31.) In times of difficulty, the bad "P" will concentrate solely on fine-tuning the product or service in order to develop something better, while the marketing and financial realities are ignored. Like salmon that only know how to swim upstream, bad product people tend to stick to what they know even when the consequences are unfavorable to their business.

CONCLUSION

Product people are inventive, talented, and passionate, but these positive traits can become weaknesses if they are left unchecked. Because product people are in love with what they do, they tend to be consumed by the product or service they provide. While this characteristic is the driving force behind innovation, it can also inhibit success when it becomes obsessive and alienating. Even the most brilliant product people may fail in business if they try to do it alone. Product people often make successful entrepreneurs, but only when they work with a strong team that harnesses their passion and creative energy.

How Does a Product Person Go Broke?

Phil was a software engineer who worked for a large company for most of his career. But when his firm was forced to downsize, Phil started his own business designing software for companies that had once been clients of his former employer. For a couple years, Phil continued to produce software programs for various companies, and business was steady. Then, one day, one of Phil's clients asked him to create a software program for a very successful specialty retail chain.

The software Phil produced was multifunctional and met many of the client's most important needs, such as invoicing, inventory control, database management, and client relations. The client expressed immediate satisfaction, and Phil realized that his product could benefit other retail chains. He did some research and found that there were approximately 5,000 specialty retailers throughout the country that could use his program. At the time, Phil's competition was limited to a single computer program that dominated the market, as retail companies had only just begun to use software systems to help run certain areas of business. This product, priced at $1,500, was far inferior to Phil's software.

Therefore, Phil was presented with an exciting opportunity. He had a product that he could sell to some 5,000 businesses at a minimum price of $1,500 each. The software could be downloaded from Phil's website or delivered directly to the business at low cost. In addition, he had the glowing testimonial of a well-known company, which considered his product the best on the market.

But what did Phil decide to do? By the time I met with him, he had already wasted a year trying to raise $1 million from potential investors. Rejected countless times, his business had started to lose money, and Phil was growing despondent. A mutual friend who knew of Phil's troubles asked me to review his business plan to figure out why investors had turned it down. I did so, and what I read was truly frustrating. Phil wanted $1 million for the sole purpose of *refining the product.* Instead of trying to sell his product to other companies, Phil wanted to essentially lock himself in his lab with other software designers and make the best product on the market—which he already had! In the end, Phil gave up his business and returned to developing software for another company.

Now having read this chapter, you may already know if you are a product person. If you are still unsure if you fall into this category, take the self-assessment test on page 33. This test contains basic questions that can help you determine if you possess the characteristics of a typical product person. If the information in this chapter does not ring true for you, marketing or financial management may be your area of strength instead. The next chapter turns to another key component in the Trinity of Management—the marketers, or "Ms" of business.

Are You a Product Person?

The self-assessment test below will help you figure out if you have the personality traits and strengths typical of product people. It is important to note, however, that this test is not meant to judge whether you are a "good" or "bad" product person. Therefore, you should also reflect upon the descriptions of good and bad product people provided in this chapter, and decide if you need to improve your attitude and become more open to working with others.

1. When people criticize your product, do you feel like they are criticizing you?

   Yes _____   **No** _____   **Not Sure** _____

2. Did it take you a long time to master your art/skill/profession?

   Yes _____   **No** _____   **Not Sure** _____

3. Would you enjoy learning your trade from a "master" in the field, even if he was strict and demanding?

   Yes _____   **No** _____   **Not Sure** _____

4. When you experience financial difficulty, do you consider developing a new product to sell?

   Yes _____   **No** _____   **Not Sure** _____

5. Do you stand by your product or service even when it does not sell well?

   Yes _____   **No** _____   **Not Sure** _____

6. Do you love to stay in your laboratory, workshop, office, or studio, shutting out the rest of the world and its distractions?

   Yes _____   **No** _____   **Not Sure** _____

7. Do you wholeheartedly agree with the quote from Steve Jobs provided at the beginning of this chapter? ("You can't just ask customers what they want and then try to give that to them. By the time you get it built, they'll want something new.")

   Yes _____   **No** _____   **Not Sure** _____

8. Are you naturally inclined, or "programmed," to try and improve the way things are made or services are delivered?

   Yes _____   **No** _____   **Not Sure** _____

9. Do you feel that your product(s) or service is the cornerstone of your business?

   Yes _____   **No** _____   **Not Sure** _____

10. Do you believe that in an ever changing world, it is important to have the next version of your product (or a follow-up product) in development?

   Yes _____   **No** _____   **Not Sure** _____

If you honestly answered "yes" to all or most of the questions above, you are a true product person. And if most of these questions did not resonate with you, it is possible that you fit the personality profile of a marketer or financial manager instead, which are discussed in Chapters 4 and 5. (See pages 35 and 45.)

4

The "Ms" of Business— Marketers

"To satisfy our customers' needs, we'll give them what they want, not what we want to give them."

—STEVE JAMES

Products and services are at the center of every business, but they must be sold in order for the company to make a profit and stay in business. For this to happen, the potential buying market must first know that the product or service exists; it must be taken to a marketplace, whether physical, virtual, or both. The individual who performs this task is the *marketer,* the driving force behind sales in a business. The marketer works on behalf of a business as well as the general public, attempting to fulfill the needs of a market by offering it the business's product or service. Marketers employ a variety of strategies and modes of communication to accomplish this goal, and their efforts affect nearly every aspect of a business, including its goals, promotional activities, advertising, branding, sales techniques, and even the company's name.

The full scope of activities involved in marketing is described well in the following quote, which has been attributed to P.T. Barnum, co-founder of Barnum and Bailey Circus: "If the circus is coming to town and you paint a sign saying, 'Circus Coming to the Fairground

Saturday,' that's advertising. If you put the sign on the back of an elephant and walk it into town, that's promotion. If the elephant walks through the mayor's flowerbed, that's publicity. If you get the mayor to laugh about it, that's public relations. If the town's citizens go to the circus, [and] you show them the many entertainment booths, explain how much fun they'll have spending money at the booths, answer their questions and ultimately, they spend a lot of money at the circus, that's sales. And if you planned the whole thing, that's marketing." Marketers must juggle all of these tasks in order to generate sales for a business, but of course, they are not all successful. This chapter takes a look at the traits and skills that make for a "good" marketer, as well as those that characterize the "bad."

GOOD MARKETERS

The primary role of the marketer is to identify the needs of a particular marketplace, and then develop and carry out a marketing plan that aims to satisfy those needs. Good marketers are able to do this efficiently and effectively because they view the world from the customer's perspective. They serve as the link between products and consumers. The good "M" matches products or services to her customers' needs in view of making the life of each client easier, safer, and/or more productive. A good marketer can even sell a refrigerator to someone in Antarctica—not because she is trying to take advantage, but because she knows that refrigerators prevent fish from freezing over. In other words, the number one priority of good marketers is to give customers what they need, want, expect, and deserve, and they are passionate about the product or service they sell when it fulfills this objective. When the proverbial tree falls in the forest, good marketers not only hear it and tell you about it, but also sell you the state-of-the-art saw that can so effortlessly chop it down.

There are a few characteristics in particular that allow them to do this successfully. First, they are highly effective communicators and careful listeners, two traits that are closely related. A good marketer is genuinely interested in customer needs and concerns beyond the business transaction at hand. Good marketers are usually outgoing as well, enabling them to make connections with others and relate well to customers. In addition, they are curious and aware of market trends; they understand what the public wants as well as what they already have and do not need. Good marketers pay close attention to patterns and shifts in the marketplace in order to generate the most sales. Another hallmark quality of good marketers is creativity, which is essential for producing original advertising, promotions, public relations, and sales strategies. They do not simply stick to traditional methods and concepts, but use their imagination to find effective and economical ways to attract the most attention and achieve the best results. This often involves employing new forms of communication. Marketers tend to quickly adopt and easily adapt to new technologies, such as mobile devices and social media. Finally, and perhaps most important, good marketers are sincere. Not only do they fully understand the product or service they are selling, but they also genuinely believe in its value. They do not use dishonest and deceptive tactics to make a sale.

In sum, good marketers bring the product to consumers with the ultimate goal of enhancing their quality of life. They are the reason grapes leave vineyards and end up in the wines you drink or the fruit bowl on your kitchen table, as well as why cars leave dealerships and enter your driveway. Good marketers facilitate the transactions that move inventions out of laboratories and into the places where they will be the most useful, whether a hospital, factory, school, office, or home. They connect the vast, dynamic, and ever-changing demands of the marketplace with the quiet, solitary, and creative world of the workshops, studios, and laboratories where new services and products are constantly being created. Without good marketing people, new technology would never be utilized and valuable services would never reach the masses. Simply put, without good marketers—skilled salespeople who are friendly, positive, energetic, and honest—the world would be an entirely different place.

It goes without saying that a good marketer is indispensable to a business. When the product person notices her products piling up around her, or when the financial manager sees low sales figures, a good marketer can step in and put a company on the right track. Still, in order for a good marketer to do what she does best—sell, sell, sell—certain parameters must be in place in the business. First, the product person in the company must be clear as to how many products can be made available at any given time. If a service is being sold, the marketer must know how many hours of work the product person can provide. Additionally, the financial manager in the business needs to tell the marketer how much money the product costs to make or the service costs to perform. Even the savviest marketer can quickly become "bad" if this information is not known or heeded. As is the case with product people, the talents of marketers are most fully utilized when the whole team works together.

BAD MARKETERS

One of marketers' most important strengths is their ability to communicate and interact with others with confidence and ease. They have "people skills" and effectively engage with customers. This type of charming personality is beneficial for a business, which must attract a clientele. But when marketers become more focused on charming consumers than genuinely trying to help them, they become "bad" marketing people. In other words, the qualities that make marketers effective can also be their downfall, leading to dishonest marketing tactics and negative stereotypes like the "snake oil salesman."

The bad marketers who are fixated on selling for selling's sake are often relentless, obsessed with making quotas, and driven by making money rather than meeting consumer needs, desires, and standards. You are probably familiar with this type of marketer. You've seen them on TV infomercials and shopping channels, car dealerships, malls, and the internet. You may even have had one knock on your front door or accost you while on vacation. These bad marketers try to sell you products or services that you neither need nor want, and sometimes cannot afford. Although they claim to "love" what they sell, their aggressiveness usually makes them seem insincere.

Even so, most of the bad marketers who exhibit these traits are not bad *people,* and most are not consciously trying to deceive customers. Like bad product people, bad marketers let their enthusiasm

Starbucks and Schultz— A Marketer's Success Story

As explained in Chapter 3, sometimes good marketers act as the impetus behind a business. Howard Schultz, now the CEO of Starbucks, is the perfect example. Born in Brooklyn in the 1950s, Schultz began his career in sales for Xerox Corporation before moving on to work for a company called Hammarplast, a Swedish drip coffee manufacturer. It was while working there that Schultz met the owners of a small coffee bean shop in Seattle called Starbucks, which had opened in 1971. He accepted a job with the business, which then had only a few locations, as their director of marketing.

During a business trip to Milan the following year, Schultz noted that coffee bars selling espresso were found all over the city. Back in the States, he proposed the idea of selling espresso at Starbucks but was met with resistance. In response, Schultz opened his own coffee shop, Il Giornale, where he sold espresso as well as coffee drinks that were also offered at Starbucks, such as the popular café latte. By 1987, Schultz had earned enough money to buy the Starbucks chain, which had grown to seventeen locations. More important, he had a marketing plan to establish and build the Starbucks brand—and he did just that.

Within less than a decade, the company had more than 1,000 locations and began to gain international recognition. By 2009, Starbucks had more than 16,000 locations and was the world's largest buyer of Fair Trade Certified coffee products. Today, Starbucks is a household name all over the world due in large part to the vision and amazing marketing ability of Howard Schultz.

The story of Starbucks shows that success is possible when marketers believe in what they sell and are determined to spread the word. Although Schultz was not the product person of the company, he was passionate about the product and knew it could be a hit if only it was taken to the mass market. With Starbucks, Schultz was selling more than just coffee; he was also selling the *idea* of a place to sit, relax, and work. The concept of the coffee café has made its way to nearly every corner of the world.

How Does a Marketer Go Broke?

Bruce had designed and produced an extraordinary catalog for Australian colonial furniture consisting of sixteen pages of glossy color photos. Each photo depicted a rare piece of furniture against the stunning backdrop of a historic Australian home. It was one of the most impressive catalogs I had ever seen.

Catalog in hand, Bruce traveled to the United States with the goal of marketing the furniture to various retailers. One salesman with whom he met offered to set up an appointment between Bruce and the company's purchasing manager in Chicago, where the central office was located. As it turned out, the company was a large American retail chain with approximately 1,200 stores across the country. The purchasing manager showed immediate interest in the furniture in Bruce's catalog and asked how many units could be delivered per week.

From an outsider's perspective, Bruce had everything going for him. But not long thereafter, a clearly uneasy Bruce came to me for advice. The reason for his anxiety was that, unbeknownst to his American client, the twelve items in the catalog were the only pieces in existence! The furniture had been handmade by a friend who had since lost interest in making furniture, as well as continuing a business partnership with Bruce. Yet the fact that the availability of the product was tenuous (to say the least) had not deterred Bruce from enthusiastically selling to one of the largest furniture retail outlets in the US. What is more, the catalog and Bruce's travel expenses had been financed entirely by credit cards to the tune of $18,000—plus interest!

In the end, Bruce went broke before selling a single piece of furniture. Not only was he alone in his business, but he also focused only on selling without considering the expenses involved or the fact that he had no one to make the product. As a result, his business venture was short-lived.

for selling get the best of them to the point that it becomes overzealous. This fervor can cloud their understanding of the marketplace or cause them to ignore it altogether. It may also result in irresponsible spending on marketing tactics, which has caused the downfall of a number of companies, notably Pets.com.

A California-based online pet supply business launched in August 1998, Pets.com had a brilliant marketing team that rolled out an advertising campaign that included television, radio, internet, and a sock puppet that quickly became a media celebrity. During the 2000 Super Bowl, the company ran a $1.2 million commercial that was later voted the most memorable commercial of the event. The problem was that the marketing team was operating unchecked by the financial arm of the company. As a result, in its first fiscal year, Pets.com earned $619,000 but spent a staggering $11.8 million, and they were out of business before the next Super Bowl.

The Pets.com story points to another hazard of unrestrained bad marketing—namely, that the desire to make as many sales as possible can lead to out-of-control spending. If a company does not have enough money or manpower to keep up with the demand of marketing and selling expenses, it will find itself in the same position as Pets.com. Of course, this problem can be avoided by having a strong team that keeps each other in line. Left alone at the helm of a company, a marketer can become too consumed by trying to sell a product or service, which may cause her to use aggressive tactics that turn off customers, use up the company's resources, or both.

This is not to say that all bad marketing starts off as well-intentioned. There are some marketers and salespeople who deliberately try to deceive customers, preying on unawareness and gullibility. These are the people who give meaning to the time-honored Latin warning, "Caveat emptor," or "Let the buyer beware." You yourself may have fallen victim to dishonest marketing practices. However, these bad marketers lie outside the scope of this discussion, which is focused on upstanding individuals who are sincerely passionate about an area of business.

CONCLUSION

Like product people, good marketers are passionate about the product or service they sell. More importantly, they are passionate about engaging with customers and providing them with something that can improve their lives. Their charismatic personality can prove to be a problem, though, if there is a lack of sincerity behind it. That is to say, marketers may become "bad" if they start to focus more on selling than on helping consumers. Although not all bad marketers are manipulative or so-called "snake oil salesmen," their aggressive tactics can turn off customers, hurting their businesses as a result. Overzealous marketing can also drain a company financially, as you saw in case of Pets.com. This is why it is so crucial that marketers work with a team. When a business has a strong team, everyone's talents are at once maximized and kept under control.

You should now have a basic idea of whether you belong in the role of a marketer. If you are still unsure, you can take the self-assessment test (see page 43), which has been designed to help you determine if you fall into this category. Keep in mind that the best fit for you may be financial management—the "FMs" of business—which is discussed in the next chapter.

Self-Assessment— Are You a Marketer?

Now that you know the skills and personality traits that characterize marketers, it's time to consider whether or not you fall into this category. By honestly answering the questions below, you can gain important insight into your suitability and effectiveness as a marketer.

1. Do you like to get to know people by asking direct questions about their likes, dislikes, and needs, and truly listening to what they have to say?

   Yes _____ **No** _____ **Not Sure** _____

2. Do you keep up with trends and developments in various industries and markets?

   Yes _____ **No** _____ **Not Sure** _____

3. Do you consider skills such as public speaking, negotiating, and customer service your areas of strength?

   Yes _____ **No** _____ **Not Sure** _____

4. Are you adept at articulating ideas and making convincing arguments?

   Yes _____ **No** _____ **Not Sure** _____

5. Are you interested in creating and implementing advertising and promotional campaigns that may include many forms of media, such as TV, radio, internet, and print media?

   Yes _____ **No** _____ **Not Sure** _____

6. Are you adept in various modes of communication, including telephones, smart phones, email, Skype, and social media?

   Yes _____ **No** _____ **Not Sure** _____

7. Do you pay attention to your appearance and attitude?

   Yes _____ **No** _____ **Not Sure** _____

8. Are you comfortable creating and taking advantage of publicity opportunities?

   Yes _____   **No** _____   **Not Sure** _____

9. Do you enjoy networking?

   Yes _____   **No** _____   **Not Sure** _____

10. Are you interested in conducting market research in order to improve or refine a product or service?

   Yes _____   **No** _____   **Not Sure** _____

If you answered "yes" to all or most of these questions and truly enjoy carrying out the tasks described above, it is likely that you are best suited to a marketing position in your business.

5

The "FMs" of Business— Financial Managers

> *"The surest way to ruin a man who does not know how to handle money is to give him some."*
>
> —GEORGE BERNARD SHAW

The third component of the Trinity of Management is the financial manager, or "FM." Since ancient times, finances have been of key importance, a fact revealed in the earliest recorded writings from ancient Babylon, which document financial transactions, accounts, and inventories. Today, financial managers play an indispensable role in business. Although FMs can be entrepreneurs, they are most often hired by business owners (product people or marketers) who recognize that handling money is not their forte.

Contrary to what many people may assume financial management is more than just understanding where numbers belong on a ledger sheet. Rather, it involves seeing and understanding the "story" that these numbers tell in order to gauge the financial future of a company. It means calculating the true cost of producing and selling goods, and making sure that a company still shows a profit after all of its expenses are added up and paid. It involves not only setting a budget and paying bills, but also piecing together the jigsaw puzzle of figures, percentages, and equations to make astute financial projections. The financial manager serves as the backbone and steady hand of a company, setting and enforcing fiscal ground rules. Without financial managers, many businesses would be in danger of sinking. This chapter will familiarize you with the multidimensional role of the financial manager, as well as highlight the key traits that can make FMs either able leaders or negative forces within a company.

GOOD FINANCIAL MANAGERS

Many struggling entrepreneurs with whom I've worked over the years have reported a feeling similar to "drowning." They felt as though they were struggling to keep their heads above water, constantly in fear that the next wave would be the one to finally finish them off. This common anxiety can be greatly alleviated by good financial managers, who help business owners navigate the often treacherous waters of business. Although he cannot stop the "the waves," an effective FM informs the business owner or CEO of the waves' height and frequency, as well as whether they should duck under the waves or ride them. To use another analogy, good financial managers are like a "GPS" for a company. They keep the business moving in the right direction, helping it to avoid potential pitfalls, surmount financial obstacles, and switch gears when necessary. They chart a profitable course for the business, steering it away from financial risk and loss.

Good financial managers possess a number of traits that allow them to excel at these tasks. For example, most FMs value order, precision, systems, and methods, and have a natural knack for numbers. As the well-known economist and former Chairman of the Federal Reserve, Alan Greenspan, once said, "It has been my experience that competency in mathematics, both in numerical manipulations and in understanding conceptual foundations, enhances a person's ability to handle the more ambiguous and qualitative relationships that dominate our day-to-day financial decision-making." Good FMs are passionate about figures, earnings, and a positive balance sheet just like product people are passionate about their specific products or services, and marketers are passionate about meeting customer needs. And also like product people and marketers, FMs are motivated not by money, but by the opportunity to help a business forge ahead and grow. They use their understanding of "profit margins," "cost of sales," "break-even points," and "cash flow" to create a clear picture of a business's financial reality in the form of financial statements, which influence company decisions. Good financial managers use current data to gain insight into a business's fiscal future.

More than this, good financial managers have a sharp business sense—they are able to see how even the most seemingly insignificant business decisions can affect the "bigger picture." A good financial manager might walk into a retail store, for example, and ask the owner why teddy bears are displayed at the front of the store. If the owner is a product person, he may reply, "Because I make them, they are the best in the world, and this shop is famous for them." A marketer may answer, "Because the public loves teddy bears, especially women. And since the shop is next door to a hairdresser, I can attract its female customers with my window display." But to these explanations, the savvy financial manager might respond, "Do you realize that you lose money every time you sell a teddy bear? An analysis of your profit margins shows that all of your profits come from selling greeting cards, which are practically hidden at the rear of the shop." This scenario illustrates one of the most important attributes of good financial managers—they can clearly see the financial reality of a business, as well as what should be changed in order to improve it. They are able to evaluate a company's finances within the wider context of the economic climate and understand its effects on the business. Their heroes are the Warren Buffetts of the world.

Good financial managers are the treasured advisors of company CEOs. They are not afraid of tackling tough circumstances or making difficult decisions. They are the surgeons of the business world, and they do not hesitate to perform a painful operation if it is the only way to restore the financial health of the company. This may involve dealing with the Internal Revenue Service or chasing down debtors to collect payment. It may mean telling product people how to properly price their products or services, or recommending that marketers stop focusing on selling products that are not generating sufficient profits. It also means keeping CEOs honest by providing them with timely and essential information—even information they may not ultimately want to hear.

With a good financial manager guiding them, product people and marketers have the freedom to focus on their jobs and do them more efficiently. However, in order to maximize the skills and talents of a financial manager, the product people and marketers must always be forthright about their department's needs, goals, and activities. The company's product people must tell the financial manager the cost of supplies and manufacturing, for example, while the marketers need to let the FM know sales quotas, advertising costs, and other related expenses.

In sum, the financial manager is a business's indispensable third leg who ensures that the company stays profitable. Good FMs estab-

John D. Rockefeller— An "FM" Entrepreneur

Although financial managers are not typically the driving force behind a business venture, there are plenty of financial management success stories. One of the most famous is that of John D. Rockefeller.

When Rockefeller began working as an assistant bookkeeper at only sixteen years old, it was immediately evident that he had a passion for finance or, as he referred to it, "the methods and systems of the office." It was this passion that led him to establish his first oil refinery near Cleveland in 1863, which grew to become the largest refinery in the area within two years. A few years later, Rockefeller founded the Standard Oil Company, which also expanded rapidly. In only a decade's time, Standard Oil practically monopolized the oil business in the United States.

Although the company was later declared by the US Supreme Court to be in violation of the Sherman Antitrust Act of 1911, its founding is a perfect example of how financial managers can also be talented entrepreneurs. Rockefeller was neither a product person nor marketer, yet he amassed a fortune based on his love of "the methods and systems of the office," as well as his shrewd understanding of all things financial.

A Financial Manager's Success Story

Kevin invented a useful wood-carving tool that he was able to produce in small batches and sell to woodworkers all over the country. He realized that his product had incredible potential, but he lacked the funds necessary to take it to the next stage of production and marketing. When Kevin asked me to help him find a source of money, I told him what he really needed first was a financial manager. He insisted that money was more important, and that if he waited much longer to raise capital, he would be forced to sell his invention to another company.

Hoping to prove my point, I organized a meeting with a prestigious venture capital firm so that Kevin could pitch his business. He gave a thirty-minute presentation during which he spoke only about his tool, while the bank executive remained silent. When Kevin was finally done, the executive looked him in the eye and said, "We don't invest in tools, we invest in people. Who are the people on your team? What is your business plan?"

As soon as we left, Kevin turned to me, embarrassed, and said, "I'm not ready, am I?" I only replied, "How can you ask for money if you don't know how much you need?" At that point, Kevin understood that he needed a good financial manager who could help him paint a picture of the size and quality of the business opportunity for prospective investors.

Through networking, Kevin met Francis, who had a strong background in finance and fit the bill perfectly. Together, they pored over figures and spreadsheets for hours. Francis was able to determine that if the business sold 25,000 tools per year, they could "cash flow" the company, meaning they could make the company grow by reinvesting profits from their own sales. He also met with Kevin's bank manager, who agreed to open a line of credit for $15,000 a month, provided that Kevin submitted copies of signed customer orders. In the first year, the business sold 50,000 tools—twice the number that was needed for the company to grow. Two years later, Kevin sold 20 percent of his business for a multimillion dollar figure. He thus paid for the company's expansion, while retaining total control of his invention and business. And none of this would have been possible without the financial acumen of Francis, who had put the company on the right track.

lish a solid financial foundation as early as possible in the life of a business, and they make sure the passion and energy of the product people and marketers are put to the best, most cost-effective use. Although their role is very much "behind the scenes," the importance of financial managers to a business should not be underestimated.

BAD FINANCIAL MANAGERS

Just like product people and marketers, the qualities that make financial managers effective can also be their demise when left unchecked. While good financial managers are always aware of the bottom line, bad financial managers believe that the bottom line is the only thing that matters in the business. They also believe that every business

How Does a Financial Manager Go Broke?

Concerned and fascinated by the environmental issues confronting the planet, Kathleen wanted to create a unique shopping experience that would educate children about nature and its fragility. Her vision came true in the form of a national retail chain consisting of 280 beautiful shops, which sold gifts and educational toys showcasing the environment. Many of these shops were situated in high-traffic locations, including high-end malls, attracting a steady stream of customers. The company's shareholders, however, complained about low-profit margins and inadequate return on their investments. The merchandise was deemed too expensive, as the products were often developed in-house by knowledgeable professionals with backgrounds in elementary education, particularly science curriculum.

Kathleen, who was adamant about maintaining the store's core "philosophy," resisted making changes, resulting in a prolonged fight with the shareholders. Eventually, Kathleen was ousted and replaced with Jacob, the CFO who had played a major role in undermining her wishes. Jacob's first priority was to restore profitability by cutting expenses wherever he could, particularly in merchandising and personnel. First, he stopped the development and man-problem is a finance problem and, therefore, tend to be insensitive and unsympathetic. Bad financial managers often do not appreciate the creative talent and passion of product people and marketers, and may belittle or ignore their needs. This may cause the company to forfeit its unique competitive advantages, such as a great product or innovative marketing approach, to concentrate on the immediate bottom line.

Although they are not representative of the majority of bad FMs, some may use their knack for numbers to "cook the books" and take advantage of people. One famous case of this type of bad financial manager is "Chainsaw" Al Dunlap, the Sunbeam executive notorious for downsizing, cutting costs, and firing people whenever he had the opportunity. And not only was he ruthless, but he was also later

ufacturing of the retailer's original toys and educational materials, as well as the purchase of high-end products. Subsequently, Jacob took a trip to China, where he found manufacturers that could produce and outsource cheaper goods at low cost.

Jacob's changes to personnel were equally profound. He eliminated the research and development team that had been assembled by the company's founder, and that remained loyal to her vision. Of greater consequence, though, was the termination of well-educated sales personnel. The ex-school teachers and biology students that had so helpfully assisted parents and children in choosing what to buy were replaced with inexperienced teenagers who were paid minimum wage. Within only one year, the once unique shops were selling generic "nature-related" items, putting them in direct competition with a huge national chain retailer, which offered similar products for the same price. It was difficult to compete with this chain, which had television promotion and could purchase inventory at steep discounts. In the end, it trounced the smaller company now being run by Jacob, who was forced to close over 100 stores just to stay afloat. Shortly thereafter, the company went out of business. In his focus on cutting expenses, Jacob completely eliminated what had made the shops special. He may have had a good understanding of numbers, but his emphasis on the bottom line ultimately caused the company's demise.

exposed as fraud who had cheated the company out of millions of dollars. More recent is the case of Andy Fastow, the former CFO of Enron who was at the center of the accounting scandal that brought down the company. These cases are extreme, but they demonstrate how greed—which can result from a fixation on numbers and money—can cause the downfall of financial officers and the businesses they manage.

In sum, financial managers fail when they focus only on the bottom line, cutting costs across the board without understanding that the real problem may lie in product development or marketing. Consequently, they can alienate, demoralize, and ultimately terminate the very people who were instrumental in creating the business in the first place. They do not understand that killing the soul of the company will essentially make them captains of ghost ships, sailing along aimlessly.

CONCLUSION

The financial manager who is truly able to see the full scope of the business can be a boon to a company. Good financial managers work with the ingredients that make a business what it is, rather than suck the life out of the company with sweeping changes based solely on numbers. Although he may not know how to build or sell a product, a good financial manager respects those who *do* have this expertise— and this is what makes the Trinity of Management work.

So now the question is, where do *you* fit in? Are you the product person, marketer, or the financial manager? And more important, do you have what it takes to excel in your role? Taking the FM self-assessment test on page 53 may lead you closer to the answer.

Self-Assessment— Are You a Financial Manager?

Once again, it's time for some self-evaluation. Do you have what it takes to be an effective financial manager of a company? Do your skills go beyond simple bookkeeping and basic accounting knowledge? By answering the questions below honestly, you will move closer to figuring out the best role for your personality.

1. Are you a detail-oriented person?

   Yes _____   **No** _____   **Not Sure** _____

2. Are you analytical and logical in the way you try to solve problems?

   Yes _____   **No** _____   **Not Sure** _____

3. Do you have a natural understanding of numbers and finance?

   Yes _____   **No** _____   **Not Sure** _____

4. Are you comfortable handling money?

   Yes _____   **No** _____   **Not Sure** _____

5. Do you get a sense of fulfillment from successfully balancing the books down to the last penny?

   Yes _____   **No** _____   **Not Sure** _____

6. Do you feel that it is important for companies to always have a clear picture of where they stand financially?

   Yes _____   **No** _____   **Not Sure** _____

7. Are you comfortable dealing with vendors, banks, and suppliers?

   Yes _____   **No** _____   **Not Sure** _____

8. Do you keep up-to-date on local economic issues that could impact a business's finances?

   Yes _____   **No** _____   **Not Sure** _____

9. Do you believe you have the leadership skills and judgment necessary to make financial decisions on behalf of a company?

Yes _____   **No** _____   **Not Sure** _____

10. Do you believe that you can tell the story of a company through their financial numbers?

Yes _____   **No** _____   **Not Sure** _____

If you answered "yes" to most of the questions above, you most likely have the personality needed to be a financial manager. Remember, knowledge and experience are acquired; it is personality above all else that enables you to excel in the financial manger position and, more importantly, perform the tasks with passion.

6

Six Common Misconceptions About Business

New businesses fail for a variety of reasons. That's a fact. But what many entrepreneurs believe about business is not always based on fact. And in a world where information is disseminated quickly and easily, these misconceptions can spread and be accepted as truth. As a result, entrepreneurs are often led down the wrong paths and doom their businesses to failure. This chapter is meant to steer you away from such misconceptions by presenting six popular "myths" of business that I have come across in my work with entrepreneurs from all over the world. Understanding the falsehood behind each of these misconceptions will allow you to make the best decisions for your business and achieve success.

MYTH #1: YOU HAVE TO LEARN HOW TO DO EVERY JOB IN A BUSINESS

As I've discussed already, one of the biggest mistakes an entrepreneur can make is to try to manage every part of their business. Some business owners take pride in the fact that they have a role in each area of their companies, describing themselves as the "chief cook and bottle washer." And it's not uncommon for an entrepreneur with this belief to expect that her team members will also learn how to do every job. This is not only unnecessary, but also counterproductive.

Of course, it's a good idea for your team to have a basic understanding of how each area of the company works. Yet, it is one thing to know the *basics* of something and quite another to be an *expert*. Sure, you can take a course in art appreciation, but will that allow you to draw or paint like a professional artist? You may be able to distinguish a Monet from a Manet, but it's unlikely you will be able to paint like either one of them. You can teach people about painting, but you cannot teach them the innate skills, personality, and passion that drive painters to do their great work. By the same token, asking the financial manager to handle marketing work, for example, is simply a bad idea, as she probably does not have the personality to communicate and engage with clients. Likewise, giving product people or marketers control over a portion of the company's financial resources is futile, not to mention potentially detrimental. It is a waste of time trying to "fit square pegs into round holes"—training team members in areas completely incompatible with their personalities, passions, and skills. Two minutes into the training lecture, their eyes will begin to glaze over. When it comes down to it, people are interested in only what they like.

One of the most ineffective things that you can do is subject one of your team members to a detailed explanation of something that she does not fully understand, care about, or need to know in order to do her job well. A server at a restaurant, for example, should know how to describe a dish, but she should not be required to know how to cook it. This, of course, is the job of the chef, who has probably dedicated several years to learning and mastering her skill. Similarly, the chef should not be required to know how to memorize orders, balance several plates of food, or remain pleasant and courteous to complaining customers. Such skills are irrelevant to their primary duties, so learning them is a misuse of time and energy.

Entrepreneurs who start businesses alone are often described as people who go from doing one thing beautifully to doing three things badly in a short amount of time. The same goes for every member of a business team. Your company will be more efficient if the product people stick to creating products, the marketers stick to communicating with the public, and the financial managers stick to overseeing expenses and expenditures. It is more important that team members respect and appreciate each other's work rather than attempt to learn how to do it themselves.

MYTH #2—THE SUCCESS OF A BUSINESS DEPENDS ON ITS IDEAS

If you are like many entrepreneurs, you may be under the impression that the key to success in business is a good idea. Many people assume that the *idea* is what drives a business, and that assessing whether or not an idea has merit is the most important thing an entrepreneur can do. After all, economic development professionals always talk about "picking winners," and they invest in businesses that they believe will outperform the competition. However, a fact that is often overlooked is that investors are more likely to believe in—and thus fund—a great business *team* rather than a great business *idea*. Too many entrepreneurs spend an inordinate amount of time trying to create something that has never been done before or improve upon a product that cannot possibly be improved. Yet, this can be a waste of time, energy, and money if you do not have a passionate, talented team.

A long time ago, I learned that businesses are not just about ideas, but the people behind those ideas. Think about it; most business ideas are neither completely original nor truly groundbreaking. There are countless Italian restaurants, clothing lines, and medical and law practices. The reason why some of these businesses succeed and others fail has little to do with whether the ideas are "good" or "bad," but rather whether the teams behind them are effective and talented. Without the right people, a business cannot go anywhere. I have seen companies sell the most trivial, useless products and become rich anyway because of the managerial skills of the people running them. On the other hand, I have heard of inventors who created life-saving devices that were never commercialized, since they lacked the skills necessary to bring them to the public.

So, is there really such a thing as a "stupid" idea in business? Allow me to answer with a few examples. First, imagine that someone tells you that she wants to sell a pebble with two plastic eyes and call it a "Pet Rock." You probably would not want her to be the product person on your team. But in 1975, an entrepreneur named Gary Dahl did exactly this: He created the Pet Rock, a seemingly ridiculous business idea. Five million Pet Rocks later, though, Dahl laughed all the way to the bank as his invention became a worldwide hit.

Big Mouth Billy Bass, a product designed by Gemmy Industries, is another example. Apparently, someone at the company decided that a singing plastic fish mounted on a piece of wood could fulfill all of Gemmy's sales dreams. The fake bass sang popular hit songs by Bobby McFerrin, Al Green, and others to the tune of millions of dollars in revenue. Once again, if someone had asked for your thoughts on the sales potential of a singing plastic fish on a wooden board, you probably would not have been optimistic.

To give you one last example, imagine if you had been the director of economic development in a small New Zealand town twenty-five years ago, and a couple of inexperienced young people told you they wanted to buy an abandoned railway bridge spanning a canyon that was 300 feet deep. And now imagine that they also told you they wanted to charge tourists to be thrown off the bridge with only a rope tethered to their feet. Most would agree that this sounds like a terrible and insane idea. But today, bungee jumping is an international industry. The sport's Wikipedia page reads, "Commercial bungee jumping began with the New Zealander, AJ Hackett, who made his first jump from Auckland's Greenhithe Bridge in 1986 . . . [and] remains one of the largest operators . . . . Despite the inherent danger of jumping from a great height, several million successful jumps have taken place." In other words, Hackett turned a very unpromising idea for a business into a lucrative industry, as well as an international phenomenon.

Stories like these discredit the idea that a successful business is the result of a brilliant idea. On the contrary, they reinforce two key business principles:

1. Business ideas are obviously important, but it is their implementation that really counts.

2. A business is more likely to make money with a well-managed "bad" idea than a mismanaged great idea.

The examples are everywhere. Consider how, every year, millions of dollars are made off of inexpensive items that are simply the latest fads in clothing, accessories, or novelty gift items. Meanwhile, products created by top university researchers often never see the light of day. All of this goes to show that a talented team that is passionate about an idea—even one that seems unoriginal or absurd—is more valuable to a business than an ingenious idea managed by a mediocre team. In business, success depends on passion, talent, and skill—and this comes from people, not ideas.

MYTH #3—YOU HAVE TO PAY TO GET HELP

It is a common misconception among entrepreneurs that they need money before they can recruit help, which is often their excuse for running their businesses alone. "I don't have money to hire anyone," they say. To this I answer, "Who mentioned money?"

You do not need money in order to find someone, or even a few people, who are willing to help you. What you *do* need is honesty and humility. By telling your friends, family, and colleagues what you want and need for your business, you will be a step closer to finding at least one person who can help you. Perhaps the second cousin of a close friend just retired from her corporate finance job and can set up an accounting system for you for free. An acquaintance may know a bright college student who is eager to lend her skills for college credits. Or you may simply find talented individuals who are willing to wait for the business to become profitable before asking to get paid for their work. Marketers, for example, are often accustomed to working on commission and will do so if they believe in your product.

In my experience, business owners who seek others to fill the key positions in the Trinity of Management usually discover that the right people for the jobs are readily available. Frequently, they personally know these individuals but never thought of asking them to help! Popular social networking websites like Facebook and LinkedIn have made it easier to connect with old friends and acquaintances, as well as other professionals in various fields. It has also made it possible to "meet" new people who have similar interests and may be of help to you as a business owner. Beg, barter, pay on commission, or offer shares in the future of the company. Do whatever you have to do to get help, just don't stay isolated.

Years ago, I met a computer scientist, Edith, a native of rural Minnesota. Edith was brilliant at her work, but her real passion was for cut flowers. She had set up a sizeable production facility on her family's farm, where she grew the flowers and dried them in such a way that they retained their color and texture for a considerable length of time. The dry roses I saw were breathtaking; she had hundreds of them displayed in her basement, where they were kept in huge cane baskets until they were taken to the local farmer's market.

Edith's main problem was that she did not like to go out and sell the flowers. A true introvert, she was not into the chit-chat, the endless niceties, and the conversations in which she had to engage with customers. She would much rather be among her flowers; in fact, I think a small part of her was actually sorry to see them sold. When I explained the Trinity of Management to her, Edith's face completely lit up, as though a light had switched on in her brain. She immediately said, "My best friend is a wonderful salesperson and was just laid off from Intel. I'm on the phone with her every day, and she is desperately trying to find something, anything, to do right now. I never considered it before, but I think she would be thrilled to help me. She'd absolutely love taking my flowers to every farmer's market in the region!"

As Edith's story demonstrates, the person you need is often right in front of you. But unless you understand who you are and what (or who) you need, you may not realize it. It's crucial for you to know not only the role that *you* play in your business, but also what roles need to be fulfilled. Once you figure this out, start looking around for help, and remember that you don't need money to get it.

At the same time, you should be cautious when going into business with people you do not know very well. A business partnership is a lot like a marriage, but getting out of it is much more difficult. So, approach business relationships like any other type of relationship.

Before entering into a legally binding partnership, get to know the other person or people, both personally and professionally, and "court" them for a long time before you "marry" them. Shared passion and enthusiasm should be enough to sustain the partnership or team; it should not be all about money. The people with whom you work should be people who share your long-term vision for the business, and are not in it simply to make money in the short-term.

MYTH #4—"STAYING SMALL" IS A POSITIVE VISION FOR YOUR BUSINESS

Many new business owners claim that they want their companies to "stay small," as though this will protect them from the risks that they believe come with growth. This claim also suggests that small businesses are easier to run, which could not be further from the truth. Just like large and midsize companies, small businesses must have a product or service to offer, which must then be successfully marketed and financially managed. Furthermore, these needs must be handled with passion and finesse in order for the business to stay in business. In reality, there is much less room for error in a small business than in a large one, which can more easily overcome financial mishaps and hardship. In a small business, one overdue payment or the loss of a single client can make all the difference. In other words, "staying small" can be riskier than growing.

Saying that you want to "stay small" often suggests that your business is already in trouble. The claim essentially sets off a warning bell to others; it raises a red flag that indicates not all is well in your company. Perhaps your business is struggling so much that a growth strategy is beyond your comprehension, and taking on more business is out of the question. The only legitimate reason for "staying small" is if your company is a hobby, side project, or something in which you are dabbling but not wholly committed to as a full-time business endeavor.

If you have convinced yourself that staying small is best for your business, consider the following questions: What will happen if you get sick and can no longer work? What will happen to your business?

What will the consequences be for your family? Unlike a job that covers sick days and provides disability insurance, a business run entirely by one person—you—inevitably suffers if you are not there to ensure it is operating properly.

I recently met an entrepreneur named Lorenzo, an Italian leatherworker in California. When he told me he wanted to keep his business small, I asked him how his family would keep food on the table if he were to get sick. Lorenzo solemnly replied, "I would be ruined." Yet, at the same time, he had a stack of orders that he claimed he did not have enough time to fulfill. He was also turning away young people who wanted to work for him just to learn the trade. I soon learned that Lorenzo's reasons for wanting to stay small went beyond financial issues; he had had a very bad experience with a business partner years earlier and, as a result, either would not or could not trust anyone else with his business. This leads me to the next common misconception among many entrepreneurs.

MYTH #5—YOU CAN NEVER TRUST ANYONE

Sometimes, people remain in business alone as means of self-protection, which may be the case for you as well. Perhaps you were burned by a business partner in the past, or watched a friend or family member go through the experience. Or maybe you have grown distrustful as a result of circumstances completely unrelated to business, such as a divorce, painful break-up, or a falling out with a friend. Whatever the cause, the idea of sharing your business with another person may seem far too risky. However, this attitude, which I call "Paranoia Central," harms a company more than it helps.

I encountered a perfect example of this attitude when I met an Australian woman named Sarah, who needed help with her business. After the initial introductions, I asked Sarah about her business idea. She quickly said, "I can't tell you that—I don't want anyone to steal my idea!" I laughed and even promised to sign a confidentiality agreement to put her more at ease, but she still refused. This kind of reaction is simply illogical; it's like going to a dentist and refusing to open your mouth, or hiring a lawyer but not telling them the reason for your lawsuit. While it's true that business ideas are secondary to the people behind them, you should still be able to communicate your ideas to others, especially prospective business partners, investors, and clients. If you voluntarily seek help for your business but refuse to share your idea—even after signing a legally binding confidentiality agreement—you probably harbor distrust for people in general, which can hurt you and your business. After all, it's unlikely that someone will want to work for a person who does not trust anyone.

If you are suspicious of others and reluctant to seek help for your company, think about your first boyfriend or girlfriend. Did you end up marrying him or her? In all likelihood, the answer is no. You may have also been depressed after the break-up, but did you give up on finding love? Didn't you pick yourself up off the floor, go out, and meet someone new? You took a risk and it paid off.

That's what life is all about. What kind of place would the world be if people could not cope with rejection, disappointment, and yes, even betrayal? What kind of place would the world be if people did not take risks or have relationships with others? Just as the end of a friendship or romantic relationship does not stop you from having new ones, one bad business partnership should not keep you from going out and finding new people to join your team. The world is filled with talented and trustworthy people; it's simply a matter of meeting them.

Over the years, I have heard numerous stories about ultimately successful entrepreneurs whose first and even second attempts at starting their own businesses were failures. In many of these cases, this was due to an untrustworthy business partner or team member. Certainly, the entrepreneurs were devastated, and they had every reason to be frustrated and angry. Some of them were forced to settle battles in the courtroom with the very people whom they had thought would be by their side for years to come. But even then, they were able to dust themselves off and move on to the next business venture—with new partners whom they trusted. They were not left demoralized, paranoid, or distrustful. In sum, businesspeople who trust others are the ones who become successful. Solitude is not only bad for the soul, but also business.

That being said, as an entrepreneur, you should not share your ideas with anyone and everyone. Get to know people, establish relationships, and if necessary, ask them to sign a confidentiality agreement. Share more with them as you become more confident in their commitment to the business. Do not resist their help, though, and do not stay isolated out of paranoia.

MYTH #6—THE BIGGEST PROBLEM FOR A NEW BUSINESS IS MONEY

Many business owners mistakenly believe that money is the solution to all of their problems. I have heard numerous entrepreneurs insist, "I don't need advice; I need money!" Of course, it's obvious that money can make running a business much easier. Yet, when it slips too easily through a company's "fingers," money can be the source of its problems as well. This frequently occurs in companies that have money but lack competent financial management.

Still, it is money, not money management, that is more popularly considered to be the cause of small businesses' financial woes. Even government officials and agencies that deal with small business start-ups emphasize the need for entrepreneurs to have more "access to finances," as though a lack of money is their only problem. It is, after all, a well-known fact that small businesses need capital, and one of the major impediments to entrepreneurial development is obtaining loans. Many would-be entrepreneurs are turned down by lenders and investors, which prevents them from starting up their businesses. Some blame this rejection on insufficient funds available for small businesses, as well as the unwillingness of lenders to take risks on small business startups.

Yet, neither of these alleged reasons is accurate. As much as $1 trillion from global capital markets is available for investing in small businesses.[1] Every single bank, including the one down the road from you, has money to lend to startups. In fact, there is more available funds than there are well-managed companies in which to invest. Investors are out there, I promise! But in order to access capital, you must first demonstrate that your business is well-managed, and that the money you receive will be used responsibly to generate profits.

Consider the situation from the perspective of the ones doing the lending—the banks, venture capital firms, micro-lenders, private investors, and so-called angel investors, which are typically affluent people who informally invest in businesses that need capital. Lenders stand to lose a potentially large sum of money if you, the borrower, mismanage it. Loaning money is especially risky for banks, which serve as the de facto trustees of their clientele's personal funds. Since they are essentially loaning out other people's money, banks must be extra cautious and selective, as well as try to minimize the risk involved. Therefore, they want reassurance that you are financially responsible, which is why you should always present potential lenders and investors with a tangible business plan. You will learn more about preparing bankable business plans in Chapter 8 (see page 83).

Unfortunately, many entrepreneurs—especially those who are inexperienced—do not realize the importance of business plans. Too many show up to meetings full of ideas about the product or service, but never address how the money they receive will be spent. As a result, their requests are turned down. After all, why would a lender want to fund a business that has no solid plan for spending money wisely and ensuring profitability?

To obtain a loan and win over investors, you must convince them that your company can manage money effectively, as well as make more of it. Having a good financial manager on your team will help you formulate a sensible, sound plan that points your business in the direction of success. In addition, here are three ways you should prepare for your meeting with prospective investors and lenders.

1. **Write your business plan with the assistance of your team.** A business plan written by one person is not worth the paper on which it is written. After all, no one person has expertise in each of the areas that a business plan should cover. Addressing your product, marketing strategy, and finances in an accurate, comprehensive manner will make your plan more bankable, as you will read about more in Chapter 8 (see page 83).

2. **Anticipate questions.** There's simply no way to avoid it: You will be asked many questions. So be sure that you and the members of your business team are prepared to respond to questions that fall into their respective areas of expertise. Together, you should be able to clearly articulate how you will take your product or service from the development stages all the way to the market, and ultimately turn a profit.

3. **Know exactly how much money you need.** Before the meeting, your financial manager should make careful financial projections in consultation with you and the other members of the business team. The person in charge of each area of the company is responsible for sharing information that may influence these projections. This will allow for more accurate figures to place in front of investors.

Of course, the risk implicit in investing and lending money is never completely erased. But by presenting potential lenders with a bankable, financially sound business plan, you can increase your company's chances of raising capital. Money problems can be greatly reduced if you demonstrate that you know how to manage it.

CONCLUSION

Common misconceptions about business, such as those discussed in this chapter, can inhibit you as an entrepreneur and hold your business back from achieving success. Letting go of these assumptions is required in order to move forward and actually start managing your company effectively. It is important that you recognize the basic idea underlying and uniting these six myths: You cannot run a business by yourself. I am tempted to stamp a warning on every new business registration form: Do not attempt this alone. You need others to help you. In the next chapter, you will find out how to find and keep a top-quality business team.

7

Putting It All Together— The Trinity of Management Applied to Your Business

For the past twenty-five years, I have worked to instill in aspiring and struggling entrepreneurs the idea that the sooner you know what your passions and skills are, the sooner you will move your business in the right direction. Knowing who *you* are and what role you play in your business is essential for making the Trinity of Management model work for your company. When you are distinctly aware of your strengths and weaknesses, you will be better able to put together a team that fulfills all of your business's most important needs—a product or service, a marketing strategy, and good financial management.

Yet, one thing is for sure: Entrepreneurs are continually seeking help for their businesses because they are not succeeding as they had hoped. About 99 percent of the time, the reason is a lack of management. Sometimes, inefficient management is the result of an entrepreneur attempting to run his business alone, despite lacking the necessary skill and passion for certain areas. In other cases, there may be a business team in place that is deficient in one or more areas, or is being micromanaged by a controlling business owner. Whatever the specific circumstances may be, inadequate management is usually responsible for the demise of a business. This chapter takes a closer look at common problems faced by struggling entrepreneurs, and presents some steps you can take to more effectively apply the Trinity of Management model to your business.

STEP 1: FIGURE OUT YOUR ROLE
IN THE TRINITY OF MANAGEMENT

When I meet a passionate entrepreneur who needs help starting a business, or running a business he is currently trying to manage alone, the first thing I do is ask him to tell me his story. Then, I grab a piece of paper and a pen, and draw the diagram I introduced in Chapter 2. (For the record, I do not claim to be a great artist.)

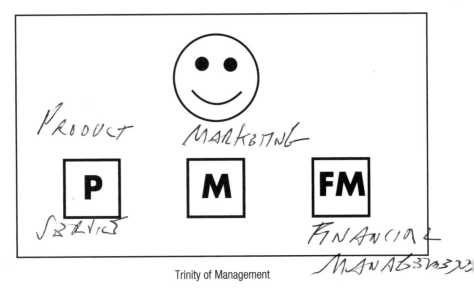

Trinity of Management

As you may recall, the smiling face represents you, the entre-preneur, while the three boxes underneath it represent the three main areas of a business. The first box (P) signifies the product or service, which is the foundation of your business—it must hold ap-peal for customers in order for the business to make money. The sec-ond box (M) stands for the company's marketing department, which must get the word out about the product or service. No mat-ter how brilliant its product, a company will fail if no one knows that it exists. And finally, the third box (FM) represents the financial management arm of the business, which works to ensure the com-pany remains profitable. If more money is being spent to make and market a product or service than the business earns in profits, the company will definitely not survive.

You already know that you need to pinpoint the area of business that matches your personality, your skills, and most importantly, your passion. If you could do what you truly love to do in your company, what would it be? Would you choose to be in the lab or studio making a product, or spending days and nights on the road trying to sell it? Or would you rather be handling financial reconciliations, entering data on QuickBooks, and making fiscal projections from the comfort of an office? In short, your first task is to figure out which box most accurately describes you. What you currently do in your company—which may be a little bit of everything— is not the issue here. Rather, you must ask yourself what you would *choose* to do if you had the opportunity to focus on only one aspect of your business. What do you *love* to do?

The responses I have received to this question are diverse, but they are always revealing and, often, regretful in tone:

- "As a farmer, my life is growing organic crops. I would love to be able to do only that."

- "I love sales and excel at it. Unfortunately, I don't have any time to actually sell to customers, since I'm too busy delivering the product and keeping bankers at bay."

- "I started this business because I had created some really outstanding and innovative software programs. But now I'm always trying to market and sell them, which is leaving me frustrated and unhappy. I don't enjoy my work anymore."

- "I wish I could do what I truly love about this company and what inspired me to start it in the first place. I love making frames, but now I spend all my time hounding debtors and paying my own overdue bills. I dread coming to work each morning because I never know what new bills I'll find!"

- "I used to be a bank auditor for a federal government agency. I really enjoyed working with a team of accountants and dealing with financial issues. But since opening my own practice, I have been struggling to find new clients. I would love to go back to dealing with numbers instead of people."

Drawing the three-box diagram and reflecting on the best fit for you is meant to trigger an "ah-ha!" moment—the moment you realize, "This is me; this is my field! This is why I started the company in the first place. This is what I do best!" As your company's founder, this is your opportunity to "hire" yourself—to do the job that you love instead of trying to fill every position in your business. Take a minute to draw an arrow linking the smiling face (you) with the box that best describes you. Now that you know who you are in the Trinity of Management, the next step is to find the right people to assume responsibility for the remaining two areas.

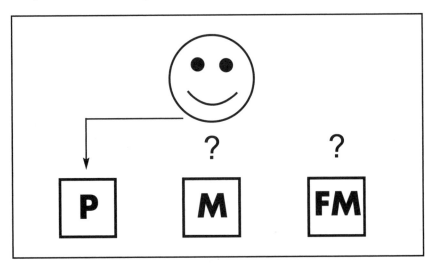

STEP 2—FIND THE RIGHT PEOPLE TO HELP YOU

As you know, each branch of the Trinity of Management must be filled in order for a business to succeed. Since you are the CEO of your business, it is your job to make sure that all three roles are fulfilled by competent, passionate individuals. For many of you, the concept of bringing new people into your company is new. I have known entrepreneurs who struggled for years, and yet never hired or asked anyone to help them. There are countless reasons why you may have found yourself steering the boat alone and bailing water from the bilges, metaphorically speaking. Excuses I hear regularly include:

- "I thought the small size of the company would make it easy to manage, so I haven't bothered to hire anyone."

- "I haven't looked for people to help me because I believed that as long as I budgeted my time, I would be able to handle it all."

- "Business isn't great; I don't have the money to hire anyone."

- "My business partners are ill-suited for their positions, or unwilling to do the work required."

- "I hired talented people, but I can't help but try to control everything myself."

I have found that this last problem, micromanagement, is especially common among entrepreneurs. Frequently, business owners act as though their employees are merely "holding down the fort" in their positions, which is another way of saying, "You handle the job until I have time to do it the right way." But this management style is never effective. It is completely counterproductive to hire people to oversee finances, create products, and come up with marketing ideas, and then overrule all of their decisions. This is just another way of trying to do everything yourself. Too many entrepreneurs are afraid to relinquish control; they believe they have to be involved in every decision, even in areas about which they know nothing or very little. Although they have a team in place, they do not let the team do what they were hired to do. It's like owning a restaurant, hiring a top-rated chef, and then constantly running into the kitchen to add salt, pepper, or some other spice to his dishes. This kind of micromanagement weakens a business. You need to trust and let others do what they do best.

Remember, the death of an entrepreneur is solitude or, to put it another way, the death of a business is a solitary entrepreneur. Look at your drawing and the two boxes that still need to be filled. Who is going to assume responsibility for these two areas of your company? If you need a marketer, ask yourself, "Who do I know in my community, or among my friends and family, that has the personality and skills to sell my product to customers?" Think about all of your options. Do you know anyone who is unemployed, underemployed, retired and willing to reenter the workforce, or simply willing to work on commission? Is there anyone whom you can trust to take on this challenge so that you can focus on your passion? You might also want to consider finding distributors, agents, or other interested parties who are willing to represent your work, such as a gallery owner. If your company lacks a financial manager, you should look for a retired accountant, bank manager, or comptroller who is looking for something to do to keep them busy.

As explained in Chapter 6, an erroneous but popular belief among entrepreneurs is that you have to pay people right away to work for your company (see page 59). This is simply not true. Instead, you must talk to people, let them see how passionate you are about your business, and tell them exactly why and how you need their help. You are likely to discover that your passion is contagious and that there are people out there who believe in your work and want to be a part of it. Very often, people do not need a guarantee of immediate financial rewards; they will want to help because you are offering them an opportunity to do what they love, to forge new partnerships and business connections, to reenter the workforce, to showcase their skills, to feel fulfilled, or all of the above. Once you find the right people, each box will be filled by a smiling face. This is the true beginning of your company. Although there is more work to be done, you now have a team ready to play the game. Before, your business was barely inside the ballpark.

One thing that is important to remember is that your business team is likely to change, perhaps several times. Different external forces push and pull companies in various directions, and sometimes personnel changes are necessary. Sometimes, business owners work with the same business team for years without realizing that it is the source of their problems. As the saying goes, they "cannot see the forest for the trees." Business owners must remember the importance of adapting to changes in the marketplace, the economy, and yes, even people. Your brilliant marketer may not be brilliant in a few years if he does not update his strategy to address changing markets, changing technologies, and changing economic and cultural climates. Of course, this does not mean that you cannot train your team members to stay on top of trends in their respective fields. But at the same time, you should not feel obligated to hold on to a team member who no longer contributes to the company, and makes no effort to boost his job performance.

It's important for you, as a business owner, to pay attention to the operations of your company and be honest with yourself if you see a problem. It's easy to become so absorbed in your work that you begin to overlook the "bigger picture." To solve this issue, I have designed an assessment tool called the "Total Quality of the Company." This assessment is a way of allowing you, the business owner, to get a better look at your company, and to evaluate each area as honestly and as objectively as possible.

STEP 3—ASSESS THE TOTAL QUALITY OF THE COMPANY (TQC)

The best way to introduce you to the Total Quality of the Company (TQC) tool is with a real-life example. Several years ago, I spoke at a seminar on entrepreneurial support in Monterey, California. Afterwards, a middle-aged entrepreneur, Ted, approached me once the room had cleared. Obviously excited, he told me that my presentation had truly resonated with him. "I'll be damned," he said. "I've been an entrepreneur all my life, but it wasn't until today that I finally understood my company's problem." He proceeded to tell me that he was the founder and owner of a company that had been in business for twenty-seven years. The annual gross turnover was $36 million, yet the company barely broke even once all expenses were paid. As a result, Ted was very worried about the future of his business.

I asked Ted if we could examine the management of his company using the TQC tool, and he accepted. On a flip chart, I drew a vertical axis like the one shown here:

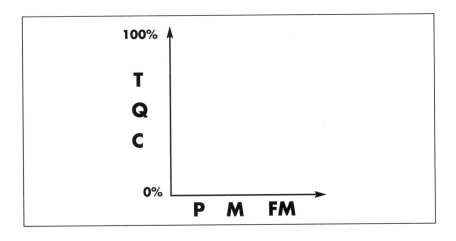

This vertical axis measures the perceived quality of each area of the business—products, marketing, and financial management—in percentage points from 0 to 100. I first asked Ted to rate his company's product: "Is your product impeccable or could it be improved? How would you grade it on a scale from 0 to 100 percent, 0 being a disaster and 100 being perfect?" Ted replied that there was always room for improvement, but overall, his company's product was very good. He rated its quality at 80 percent. I could tell he was being honest, so I made a mark at the 80-percent line on the vertical axis, as shown below:

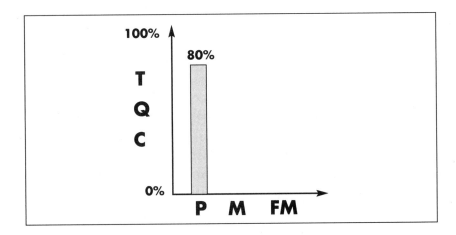

I then asked Ted to rate the quality of his company's marketing strategy using the same scale. He believed this part of his business was also very strong, as it had gained many loyal clients and was steadily drawing in new ones. He gave the marketing department a grade of 80 percent as well, which I marked on a second drawing:

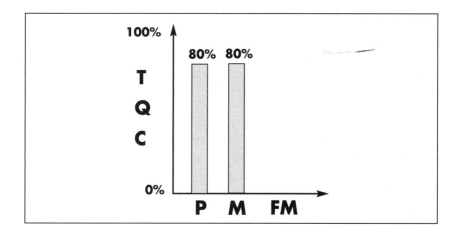

Now I was rather curious about the source of the company's problems. Since two of its areas were apparently performing very well, could financial management be the weak link? And if so, how big of a weakness was it? I soon got my answer. When I asked Ted to rate the quality of his business's financial management, his response was worse than I had expected: "At best, 20 percent." I was stunned. How could he allow his company, which made $36 million a year, to be so poorly financially managed?

"Who is in charge of finances?" I asked.

He replied, "Me! I have a CEO, bookkeepers, and accountants, but I never let them make financial decisions. I always meddle in it. I don't know what I'm doing nor do I like doing it." He also admitted, "I am the source of the company's financial misery. Without knowing what I was doing, I renegotiated the leasing agreement for our fleet of trucks, and nearly sent the business into bankruptcy." Then Ted told me that my presentation had helped him vividly "see" his company's problem for the first time. Taking the marker from my hand, he drew a large arrow shooting upwards from the 20-percent line on the third diagram I had drawn. Confidently, he said, "I am going to partner up with my CEO and go headhunting for the best CFO we can find."

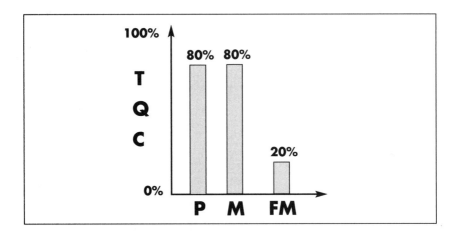

The word Ted continually used to describe how the presentation had helped him was "see." The diagrams I used during both the seminar and our conversation made it clear to him where his business was falling short. This is why the TQC approach is so valuable, especially for people who are very visual in how they think, perceive, and learn. I have found that this series of simple visual aids allows entrepreneurs like Ted to gain clarity and insight into a situation that had previously seemed very muddled and confusing.

Using the TQC approach to assess your business can be highly effective, no matter how big or small your company. For instance, I successfully applied the TQC to the public works department of a large British city. The department had recently downsized its workforce from 4,000 to 1,500 employees. But this change had not disrupted its services, and had actually saved the city a considerable amount of money. Nevertheless, the public viewed the department very negatively, and the management team wanted to know how and why this perception had developed.

I asked the CEO and the managers to grade the quality of the department's service, marketing, and financial management. The diagram resulting from their combined ratings looked like this:

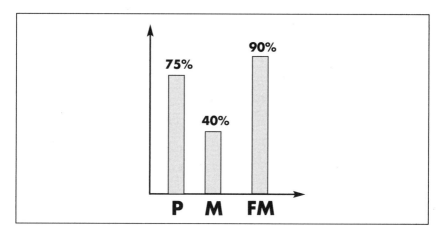

The department's managers told me that the engineers (product people) were doing a good job, and that the accountants (financial managers) were at the top of their game. They were given grades of 70 percent and 90 percent, respectively. However, as you can tell from the diagram, the department apparently lacked strong marketing. In fact, as I soon found out, they had no internal marketing and communications staff! Since there was no one to convey to the residents that the cuts had saved the city a significant sum of money, as well as that there was great progress being made, it was no wonder that the department's public image had suffered. The managers explained to me that they had been using outside public relations firms to communicate with the public, but only when necessary. They immediately recognized that the department would be better serviced by implementing their own marketing team, since recent events had shown that erosion of public trust could undermine all of their good work.

If you work with a business partner or team, I encourage you to create TQC diagrams independently of each other. These drawings are often truly revealing, as people within the same company can have completely different perceptions of its management quality. I once asked a husband and wife team to assess their struggling business using the TQC method. Here are the separate drawings the two of them produced:

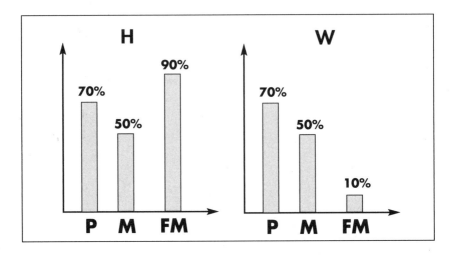

Although they agreed on the quality of the product and marketing, their views of the company's financial management could not have been more different, as the diagrams illustrate. While the husband thought its quality was excellent, his wife felt it was pitiful.

When the husband saw his wife's drawing, he was puzzled and caught off guard. "You gave our financial management a rating of 10 percent? What do you mean?"

His wife replied, "I am in charge of the finances, and I have no clue what I'm doing! I absolutely hate doing it. The only reason I am trying to take care of the money is because *you* don't want to do it!"

At that moment, this husband-wife team realized that their business was not being financially managed at all. They were a product person and a marketer trying to handle money issues without really grasping the financial implications of their decisions. As is so often the case, two simple TQC diagrams can start a difficult conversation— but one that is necessary to the health and longevity of your company.

Of course, using the TQC tool does bring up some questions. You may be wondering what happens when a company's product person, for example, rates the product at 80 or 90 percent, when a more accurate grade is more like 20 percent? In other words, how do you know you and your team are being honest and objective?

The solution is to simply follow the Trinity of Management, which is self-correcting when it is properly applied. An entrepreneur who works alone can exaggerate his product or skills, but not one who works in a team. The Trinity of Management is based on the idea that a business is the sum of its parts, and that each area of a company has an impact upon the others. In addition, there is a built-in system of checks and balances that holds every person accountable for the job they perform. In this way, the TQC tool is essentially fool-proof. A marketer cannot give himself a grade of 80 percent, for instance, if the financial manager has records showing that sales are dropping. Likewise, a product person cannot rate his performance at 90 percent if the marketer reports customer dissatisfaction. When there is a team, everyone keeps each other in line, thereby preventing skewed TQC assessments. Over the years, I have met many entrepreneurs who worked alone and gave themselves inflated evaluations, despite the fact that their companies were floundering. But I have never met a business team in the same circumstances that exaggerated its performance.

Let me give you an example. A client, Jim, came to me seeking assistance with a new business venture. A certified public accountant (CPA) by profession, Jim now wanted to set up a compost business in Western Australia selling processed organic manure to nurseries and commercial vegetable growers. His brother-in-law had recently established this type of business in Eastern Australia and had thus far been very successful. Jim had already sourced a group of pig farmers, and entered into an agreement to process and sell their processed manure under the brand name popularized by his brother-in-law's company. He had also put up his house as collateral in order to acquire a bank loan in the amount of approximately $200,000 (in Australian currency). But because Jim was a financially smart CPA, he also wanted to locate a low-interest source of funding in order to minimize debt, and he approached me for advice.

I told Jim that if his business was as promising as he believed, he would be able to find an investor or even a minority shareholder to bankroll the company startup. This would require him to create a business plan that covered the three main areas of the company. First, the plan needed to demonstrate the virtues of the product, which Jim rated at 90 percent on the TQC scale. He was confident that the product was top-quality, and there was plenty of data on his brother-in-law's company to support this view. Preparing financial documentation—another crucial element of the business plan—would also not be a problem, Jim told me, since he was a CPA. He gave his financial management skills a grade of 100 percent. Finally, Jim would have to show investors that his product had *market acceptance,* or sales potential. To accomplish this, I recommended that he hire a marketer to acquire letters of intent to purchase from possible customers, such as nurseries and commercial growers. However, Jim believed that market research was unnecessary due to the fact that the product had sold so well for his brother-in-law's company. Plus, he was in a hurry to begin production, and conducting research would only delay the process. I finally convinced him to employ a student from a local agricultural college to do the job. This way, Jim would get valuable information to help reassure investors without having to pay a large sum of money to a marketing professional.

Jim was optimistic about results, so he experienced quite a shock when the student reported his findings a month later. According to the student's research, not a single nursery or commercial grower wanted the product. How could this be? Jim had been extremely confident in the product's ability to sell, considering his brother-in-law's success in Eastern Australia. The poor results of the market research left him confused and frustrated.

Jim soon realized why the product, processed compost, had little to no sales potential in the region. First, Western Australia had a thriving trade in live animal exports. The manure left by the animals, which were held in the ports before boarding ships, was given away by the Port Authority to anyone who was willing to take it off the property. Nurseries and farmers, therefore, could obtain compost at no cost. Second, commercial vegetable growers in Western Australia had recently invested in a massive factory that produced a powerful fertilizer—liquid urea—that was pumped to the fields or applied directly to the crops. This method was usually preferred to using solid compost, which was a major hassle to transport. As a result, Jim was out of business before he was actually *in* business. The market research had clearly demonstrated that even an excellent product that is successful in one market can fail in another. More importantly, it had taught Jim the value of the TQC tool, as well as the Trinity of Management in general. Had he not agreed to do some marketing, Jim would have gone into business ignorant of the fact that there was no market for his business in Western Australia—and the consequences might have been truly damaging, financially and otherwise. His experience, though unfortunate, illustrates the potential pitfalls of a quality gap in a company, as well as how correcting the imbalance can put a business on the proper track.

In sum, a team is essential for figuring out the TQC of your company. Left unchecked, product people can become fixated on their product or service, and spend all of their time, energy, and money on researching and developing it to the detriment of other company needs. Marketers may try to make a sale and gain popularity with clientele, regardless of the cost and by whatever means possible. Financial managers might start paying attention to only the bottom line, cutting costs wherever they can until they are left with a company that barely resembles the original dream.

In the existentialist drama *No Exit* by Jean Paul Sartre, hell was three people in a room. In business, however, hell is one person in a room. It takes all three players—product person, marketer, and financial manager—for a company to compete in the game of business. It is of utmost importance that you understand that if you do not let others in your "room," it is going to be extremely difficult to become a successful entrepreneur. It's interesting to note that the word "company" was originally used to refer to people with whom you "broke bread," or ate. In other words, although it is singular, "company" actually implies the plural—there is no company of one.

CONCLUSION

Every business is bound to encounter difficulty and conflict. Product people, marketers, and financial managers view the world in fundamentally different ways, and this can cause disagreements. The metaphor that continually comes to mind when describing the dynamics of a business team is marriage. A marriage is essentially the act of two individuals with different backgrounds, personalities, and genetics teaming up to share a life together and, very often, to start a family. But how much work is needed to keep the relationship strong? Plenty! Like successful married couples, a successful business team must know how to listen, compromise, and respect the others' opinions. Furthermore, the most successful couples are those whose skills and personalities complement each other, thereby allowing them to work well as a team. For example, one might handle the finances, while the other performs home repairs; one might plan and organize family vacations, while the other packs and drives the car. This cooperative effort must also be active in a business. Just as people have certain roles in a marriage or family, so too do members of a business team. And when every person knows his part and does it well, the business can succeed.

8

Your
Bankable Business Plan

In the UK, there is a popular reality television show called *Dragons'
Den*, which revolves around entrepreneurs pitching ideas to four
or five merchant bankers—the "dragons"—who then decide if they
want to invest in the business. While this may seem like a harmless
premise for a TV show, it is often uncomfortable to watch. Each entrepreneur, standing alone in front of the panel of bankers, is asked
questions specifically targeted at her weaknesses rather than her
strengths. If she is a strong marketer, she will be asked questions about
finances. If she is a talented product person, she will be quizzed mer-
cilessly about branding and advertising. As a result, the entrepreneurs
are reduced to sweating, rambling fools in a matter of minutes. It's as
cringe-worthy as the scene in *Gladiator* in which Commodus, the film's
villain, stabs Maximus—the hero played by Russell Crowe—before
the actual fight even begins. Like Maximus, these entrepreneurs never
stand a chance.

Dragons' Den may be a hit, but watching the show only makes me
want to help the entrepreneurs get their acts together, find alternative
sources of funding, and ultimately, have the last laugh. How would
I prepare these entrepreneurial "gladiators?" Well, for starters, I
would tell them never, *ever* to enter the "arena" alone. You should
meet with investors only after forming your team, and all members
should be at your side at the meeting to answer questions related to
their respective fields. Additionally, I would make sure the entrepre-

neurs went in armed with a tool just as important as their team: a bankable business plan.

When you approach a bank, economic development agency, investor, or other source of financial backing, the first thing you will be asked to produce is a business plan. Business plans are used as part of a screening process to "weed out" undesirable clients. "Come back when you have a business plan," is a common dismissal of entrepreneurs who seek investment capital before they have formally outlined plans for their businesses. But what investors should say instead is, "Come back when you have a team." Business plans and business teams go hand-in-hand, as you need a Trinity of Management—product people, marketers, and financial managers—to create a plan that is well-rounded and *bankable,* or likely to produce financial gains for the company. This is inherent in the Trinity of Management philosophy and is explained further in the first part of this chapter. The subsequent parts cover the three key components of effective business plans—product, marketing, and finance—so that you can begin writing a plan that puts your business firmly on the road to success.

THE TRINITY OF MANAGEMENT AND BUSINESS PLAN WRITING

Giving advice to small businesses has become a huge industry, and teaching entrepreneurs how to write a business plan is both its "sacred cow" and cash cow. Most of the time, it's expected that entrepreneurs will singlehandedly write their own plans. It's not uncommon for business counselors, course instructors, and economic development officers to have entrepreneurs fill out blank business plans that follow a basic template. But this approach only sets entrepreneurs and their businesses up for failure.

Ned, an economic development officer in Chicago, learned this lesson the hard way. He told me, "After hearing [you] speak at a conference [about the Trinity of Management], I went home depressed. That night I kept thinking about all the entrepreneurs who had come to me over the years wanting help with their business ideas. I had always just given them blank business plans to fill out. I never saw them again!" Ned realized that he had been setting these entrepreneurs up for disaster by expecting them to write a business plan entirely on their own. Unfortunately, this expectation is the cause of much frustration, stress, and shattered dreams among prospective business owners. They may lose self-confidence and ambition, drop out of business school courses, and give up on their ideas. They fall victim to the erroneous belief that a good entrepreneur must be able to singlehandedly write a business plan. What nonsense!

Let there be no confusion: Entrepreneurs cannot and should not write a business plan by themselves. Businesses are multifaceted and so are business plans. As I have stated repeatedly throughout this book, no one is adept in all three areas of the Trinity of Management. And in order to write a sound business plan, you need a team of experts who are just as passionate and motivated as you are. You should direct most of your efforts towards writing the part of the business plan that falls into your area of expertise and let your team take care of the other parts. In other words, act like a focused laser beam in your company, making your area of expertise shine like a jewel; do not be a dull fluorescent light attempting to illuminate the whole company.

Because your plan should accurately and thoroughly describe your product or service, you need a product person; because it must outline your company's strategy for selling the product, you need a marketer; and because your plan must also convince investors that your business will be lucrative, you must find a financial manager. In other words, unless your plan is a collaborative effort, it is barely worth the paper on which it is written, no matter how long or intently you have worked on it. This is what I tell my clients as they prepare for meetings with investors, and the outcomes have been overwhelmingly positive. In one instance, a venture banker decided to invest his *own* money—not his firm's—in my client's business! You can find yourself in this same scenario by presenting investors with a three-tiered business plan, which is outlined on the following pages.

PART 1: THE PRODUCT OR SERVICE DESCRIPTION

Written by the company's product person, the first part of your business plan should outline the main aspects of the business's product or service:

1. The innovativeness and usefulness of the product or service.

2. Proof that the product or service can be protected from potential imitators. This includes patents, copyrights, and any other legal documentation demonstrating that you control the technology, name, or other aspects of the product or service.

3. The qualifications and experience of the company's product people.

The product portion of your plan should not be hundreds of pages long. An appropriate length is anywhere from three to fifteen pages depending on the complexity of the product. Any supplementary material—test results, drawings, and charts, for example—can be submitted as addendums. Basically, prospective investors and lenders want to know what makes your product unique and distinguishes it from other products (or services) that may be similar. Even if your idea is not completely original, investors want to see that it offers some new, distinct benefits for consumers. And if your idea is brand new, they want to make sure that it is legally protected so that they do not lose money should they decide to invest.

Finally, investors are typically interested in *who* is developing, manufacturing, or delivering the product or service. This is also why it is so important to have qualified, experienced, and talented individuals on your team—investors can be swayed by a team that exudes passion and expertise. For example, if you are opening a restaurant, mention that your head chef, manager, or maître d'hôtel have been successful in the past. Noting the achievements of your team can make all the difference between a boring proposal and one that inspires confidence in the investors.

The product person's part of the plan should reflect both her passion and her expertise, making her less vulnerable to intimidation by the panel of "dragons" reading it. At the same time, it's important that her expertise not make the plan difficult to understand. Sometimes, highly specialized products—such as a piece of cutting-edge technology or medical-related service—are difficult to explain in layman's terms. As a result, the product section of a business plan can become filled with technical jargon or unfamiliar terminology that may confuse or turn off those who are reading it.

If the technology involved is very complex, such as in medical research or nanotechnology, you may want to find investors who specialize in your field and will understand your presentation. Alternatively, consider seeking help from a professor or other professional in the field who is able to clearly explain the technology, as well as vouch for its soundness. I recall one young inventor who asked a nuclear physicist to review and give feedback on his electrical rust-proofing device before approaching investors, which worked to his advantage and prepared him better for the meeting. If you have developed the product, you probably already know who your peers are and can approach one of them to help you.

If you cannot find the appropriate person to assist you, it may be necessary to hire a professional scientific writer or advisor who can translate very technical or complicated plans into reader-friendly language. Keep in mind that bringing in outside help can be expensive, so this should not be your first course of action. You can always ask family members or friends to read the product portion of your plan to see if they understand it. Sometimes, all it takes is asking to get a highly valuable source of help.

PART 2: THE MARKETING PLAN

The marketing component of the business plan is written by the marketer on your team and is divided into four main parts:

1. Qualifications and experience of the marketing director or manager

2. Explanation of the marketing strategy

3. Competitive analysis

4. Letters of intent to purchase written on company letterheads

The first section is used to introduce the person in charge of the marketing plan and establish her competency. If you are opening a restaurant in Las Vegas with a circus theme, for example, and the marketing director once worked in marketing for Cirque du Soleil, you should say so! One thing that new entrepreneurs do not often realize about business is that the personal expertise of the individuals running a company is highly valuable. I remember a banker telling me that he would be prepared to invest millions of dollars in a company if one particular individual he knew joined the business team. Some of the best advice for you as an entrepreneur is to use past work experience, academic credentials, and any other indicator of the marketer's qualifications to persuade investors.

The second section is meant to identify, define, and describe your market. This part of the plan should state who your customers are, and the products or services they want, need, and expect. It should also indicate how much money they are most likely willing to spend on the product or service. In addition, you must explain how you will go about selling your product, specifying your channels of distribution and marketing methods. You should say if you plan to utilize print advertisements (such as in newspapers and magazines), social media, TV and internet, seminars, online workshops, or all of the above. If you have sufficiently established your marketer's credibility, investors should be confident in your choice of strategy and its ability to maximize market penetration.

As its name suggests, the *competitive analysis*—the third section of the marketing plan—identifies your main competitors in the target market, as well as their strengths and weaknesses. Here, you should state the benefits of the competing products or services, how much they cost, and how your product or service is superior. In other words, you need to prove that your business will establish itself as a strong competitor in the market. This part of the plan demonstrates that your marketer has done her homework by knowing who the competition is and how your business will outperform it. This section should not go on for pages and pages, but should sufficiently show that (1) you have researched businesses similar to your own, and (2) that yours has the competitive edge.

The last section of the marketing component of your plan moves beyond planning, strategy, and analysis. Now you must present tangible evidence of your product's *market acceptance,* or its ability to sell in the intended marketplace. Prior to showing your plan to investors, your marketer should visit possible clients, provide them with a sample of your product or a description of your service, and determine their level of interest in using it. If they express enthusiasm, your marketer should ask them to put it in writing in the form of a *letter of intent to purchase.* She should be clear that it is not a financial or legal transaction, but only an indication of the client's interest in purchasing the product (or service) if it is delivered at the price and standards described. Letters of intent to purchase should be written on company letterhead and signed by an authorized company representative. You should acquire as many letters of intent as possible, which will depend on the size of your market and company, as well as the kinds of products or services you sell.

At this point in the plan, you will have described your product to a tee and shown that you have a plan for selling it. You will also have demonstrated knowledge of your competitors, as well as how you can surpass them. Furthermore, you have concrete proof of your product's marketability to place in front of potential investors and lenders. But remember, no matter how great the product or marketing strategy, your business plan still must demonstrate your company's ability to make a profit. This leads us to the third fundamental aspect of your bankable business plan.

PART 3: THE FINANCIALS

Certainly, prospective investors are going to question the financial plausibility of your business plan. Once again, we will call upon the person best qualified to answer such questions—your financial manager. The FM must prepare all required financial statements using standard accounting procedures. These statements fall into four main categories:

1. Estimates of startup costs

2. Projected balance sheet

3. Projected income statement for twelve months forward

4. Projected cash flow for twelve months forward

The above statements must be audited by a certified accounting firm—the more reputable and well-known the firm, the better. The audited statement should be printed on the accounting firm's official letterhead, and appropriately signed and sealed. It's especially important that it is placed last the business plan, as it is a well-known fact that investment bankers tend to open business plans from the back to assess the company's potential for profitability. It's crucial that the first document they see is an independent audit statement affirming that all enclosed financial statements are based on data that can be verified. An independent audit reassures investors that the figures upon which the business plan is based are sound. Of course, the numbers are still only projections, but when combined with other material in the business plan—market research and letters of intent to purchase, for example—this information can boost investors' confidence in your business.

Naturally, the credentials of your chief financial officer should also be stated somewhere in this part of the plan. Education, related work experience, and any professional licenses or memberships should all be mentioned. Since financials are of utmost importance, your CFO should be highly qualified—especially if you are asking investors for a large sum of money.

FINALIZING YOUR BUSINESS PLAN

Your bankable business plan is nearly ready. Once the three main parts have been drafted—the product or service description, the marketing plan, and the financials—you can start to write your executive summary. The *executive summary* (ES) is a concise synopsis of your plan's key points. Its goal is to interest and even entice the reader by outlining the fundamentals of your business. Be careful that you or whoever writes this section does not focus too heavily on any one area of the business, but includes an equal amount of information on each section. In total, your executive summary should be between one and two pages.

When your plan is complete, you should have it organized, collated, and indexed. Supplementary material—such as diagrams, charts, or patents—should be submitted separately. The full business plan (not including the letters of intent to purchase) should be no more than forty-five to fifty pages in length.

Remember, there are countless business plan templates available for free online. These can be valuable resources and guides, but keep in mind that content is more important than form. Your first priority should be addressing the concerns of your readers—the investors.

CONCLUSION

There is a wide range of opinions among business professionals regarding formal business plans. Yet, this does not negate the fact that your business plan weighs heavily on the future of your business. You need a business plan in order for investors to take you seriously, and you need a team to help you write it. As I have emphasized throughout this book, successful entrepreneurs understand that effective management goes hand-in-hand with a division of labor. As you go forth in your business endeavors, remember that you need a plan that is well-rounded, financially sound, and a team effort.

Although this chapter provides key guidelines for making your business plan bankable, you may wish to provide your team with templates to help write and organize the plan. The appendix (see page 107) recommends business plan writing guides that can serve as valuable resources for you and your team.

9

The Social Aspect of Entrepreneurship

Social interaction is one of the most important aspects of business. More than technology, university degrees, and efficient office setups, interpersonal connections help businesses succeed. As I have argued throughout this book, people form the backbone of companies, and *who* you know is just as important as *what* you know when it comes to transforming your vision of a business into reality. I can tell you countless stories about entrepreneurs who achieved success after finding the right people to help them learn, brainstorm, and build a business team. I can also share stories of investors and other financial backers who said "yes" to projects not simply because of the product or service, but because they believed in the individuals sitting across the table from them. As this chapter reveals, social connections among individuals lie at the forefront of entrepreneurial success.

THE IMPORTANCE OF BEING SOCIAL

You are well aware by now that a team is essential for starting a business—despite the fact that entrepreneurship is often viewed as an independent act. My firm belief in this approach to business management has been greatly influenced by two highly regarded professors who have done extensive research on the topic of what makes entrepreneurs successful. Their work, which I will share with you, can help shed light on the social nature of business.

One of these professors is Per Davidsson, the Director of the Australian Centre for Entrepreneurship at Queensland University of Technology (QUT). He has written that "entrepreneurship is much more a social game than an individual one. The most striking characteristic of a successful entrepreneur is perhaps the ability to identify, cultivate, and use other people's competencies."[1] His work supports the popular claim that "who you know is just as important as what you know." He and his research partner, Benson Honig, conducted a study on individuals involved in startup enterprises, following them over an eighteen-month period. The study, entitled "The Role of Social and Human Capital Among Nascent Entrepreneurs,"[2] used firsthand observations of businesses instead of subjective accounts and memories of entrepreneurs who had already become successful.

Davidsson and Honig first examined the role played by *human capital*—the value of individual education and skill—in the businesses. They found that individuals who possessed technical skills and had several years of schooling in their area of expertise started businesses at a higher rate than those who did not. Still, there was no evidence indicating that these individuals would succeed any sooner than entrepreneurs who did not have the same level of preparation. Next, Davidsson and Honig assessed the businesses' *social capital*—namely, the bonds between the entrepreneurs and their business teams, external business networks, and even families and friends. They concluded that the entrepreneurs who had both strong business networks and tight family bonds were consistently more capable of making early sales and showing profits than those who did not participate in these types of social interactions.

All of these findings surprised the researchers, who did not expect to see that social interaction helped businesses succeed more so than individual education and training. Davidsson went on to study thousands of entrepreneurs in the early stages of their ventures. He consistently found that social capital proved more influential in the success of a business than human capital. He determined that one way for entrepreneurs to minimize business risk is to belong to business networks, service clubs, and other organizations that enable the exchange of business information and advice. Perhaps his most important finding is that even superficial social interactions can have a profound effect on a new entrepreneur. A casual conversation with a friend, for example, can throw a completely new light on a business and shape its future direction. In other words, social connections matter in business, and individuals who reach out, ask questions, and remain open and curious are more likely to succeed.

TEACHING ENTREPRENEURSHIP

The second of the two professors I first mentioned on page 93 is Saras Sarasvathy, a former pupil of Nobel Laureate and economist Herbert Simon, and a highly accredited associate professor from the Darden School of Business at the University of Virginia. In her quest to discover "what makes entrepreneurs entrepreneurial,"[3] Professor Sarasvathy interviewed successful entrepreneurs with the aim of discovering whether or not there was a common "core" to how they operated. She essentially wanted to find out if such a thing as "entrepreneurial thinking" existed, and if entrepreneurs thought and solved problems in a similar fashion.

Professor Sarasvathy posed hypothetical questions to dozens of successful and well-established entrepreneurs in her attempt to uncover the secret of entrepreneurial reasoning. She discovered that entrepreneurs have a particular way of looking at the world. For lack of a better word, she called their way of reasoning "effectual"—the opposite of *predictive,* or *causal, thinking.* Causal thinking assumes that if you know what you want, you are likely to achieve it because you can control the outcome by using whatever means are at your disposal. According to Sarasvathy's findings, however, entrepreneurs generally do not think this way. In fact, the entrepreneurs whom she interviewed had no specific goals or outcomes that they wanted to reach upon starting their companies; they were more like explorers setting out in unchartered waters to discover new worlds. In Sarasvathy's words, "Where managers say: to the extent that we can predict the future we can control it, entrepreneurs say: to the extent that we can control the future we do not need to predict it." Like explorers, concluded Sarasvathy, entrepreneurs do not have plans or expectations, but use all tools at their disposal and any help they can find to reach "habitable land." Only when they find the "land" do they start thinking about how to develop, establish, and manage it.

Sarasvathy deemed this kind of thinking "effectual" to clearly differentiate it from causal reasoning. However, as she points out, business students are often trained in causal thinking: "In our classrooms, we teach potential entrepreneurs an extremely causal process—the sequential progress from idea to market research, to financial projections, to team, to business plan." Furthermore, in business school, entrepreneurs-in-training are rarely taught how, as Davidsson says, "to identify, cultivate, and use other people's competencies." In Sarasvathy's words, "As far as I know, no entrepreneurship programs offer courses in creating and managing lasting relationships or stable stakeholder networks." Basically, what is taught about entrepreneurship is often at odds with the inclinations of most entrepreneurs, not to mention business in general.

Sarasvathy's discoveries perfectly match the findings of Per Daviddson—namely, that successful entrepreneurs tend to start small and use the resources immediately at hand, including people they know and trust. According to Sarasvathy, the entrepreneurs who participated in her study were open, smart, and able to pick others' brains, as well as tap into a variety of available resources. They did not shy away from advice or the opinions of others, but actually sought them out; they were very happy to associate with potential helpers. Academic studies and biographies of entrepreneurs alike seem to confirm that business is essentially a social event, and that learning how to build and maintain relationships should be a primary concern of anyone who wishes to start a business. But in order to cultivate these skills, you must first let go of the myth of the solitary entrepreneur—the "rugged individualist" or triumphant hero who "goes it alone"—and replace it with a new business vision that truly reflects the reality of entrepreneurship.

Joseph Campbell, author of the acclaimed book *The Hero with a Thousand Faces*, offers interesting insight into the subject of heroes and what makes them successful. He explains how nearly every culture seems to treasure and recount stories of courageous individuals who embark on challenging journeys. But he also points out a very important—and often overlooked—detail that these heroic accounts share. He eloquently writes, "Once you have crossed the threshold, if it really is your adventure—if it is a journey that is appropriate to your deep spiritual need or readiness, [then] magical helpers will come along the way." What a revelation! Not even the classical "hero" overcomes obstacles and attains success alone. There are plenty of stories in our own culture that support this idea. Just think of Dorothy from *The Wizard of Oz*. Would she have made it home without help from the Scarecrow, the Tin Man, and the Cowardly Lion—her "Trinity of Management?"

It seems that the current mythology should be replaced with a concept that is closer to the reality of entrepreneurship. The heroic entrepreneur should be one whose success is the result of personal courage as well as social connections. After all, it is only when you are open to finding and being found by others that your "magical helpers" will appear.

FINDING YOUR TEAM

In previous chapters, I have suggested ways you might go about finding people to help you with your new business. But let's imagine that you are new to your community and have no business contacts. You are, in other words, truly isolated. Where do you go to find your product person, marketer, or financial manager?

Years ago, my business partner, Nick, and I were looking for a financial manager for our company. I was new to town at the time, so I contacted a local business association to find out if they held networking meetings. They did not, but they were able to refer me to a group of retired business executives who met on a regular basis. I attended one of these meetings and met Gareth, a former banker who had been recruited by the federal government to audit banks during the savings and loans crisis of the 1980s and 1990s. Afterwards, he had started his own accounting and financial management firm but, as I soon discovered, still worked alone. During our conversation, I commented that it must be difficult for him to find clients without a marketer to help him. He appeared startled and replied, "Absolutely! I don't have enough clients. But where can I find a marketer? I have at least 400 former colleagues, but they are all in accounting and finance. I have no idea how to go about finding someone to market my service." We began working together shortly thereafter.

The reason I bring up this story is because it is an example of the *habitat idea* in action. The habitat idea simply means that likeminded people tend to congregate in the same place, or "share the same side of the forest." If you see one financial manager or marketer, there are probably many more nearby. You should keep the habitat idea in mind as you embark on your search for business team members. To find a financial manager, for instance, you must find the closest habitat of people who deal with money on a daily basis. Visit the local bank, credit union, or even the finance team at a church or school, and ask to be referred to someone who may be able to help you in your business. This same rule applies to finding marketers. If you can get the name of a marketer at a business nearby or in a university's marketing department, it's very likely that he will know others in the same field who can be of service to you. Yes, it's true that birds of a feather flock together: Doctors can recommend doctors, mechanics can recommend mechanics, and writers can recommend writers. People within the same discipline tend to know each other, as well as other "habitats" in which they commonly congregate and communicate.

Today, the internet allows you to explore multiple "habitats" without ever having to leave your house. It is a treasure trove of specialized networks and professional associations. But be careful; while it can be a great resource for meeting people and getting leads, the internet is also unreliable because of the anonymity it allows. Years ago, when the internet was still in its early stages, a telling cartoon was printed on the front page of a major publication. The cartoon depicted two dogs sitting at a desk in front of a computer with the caption, "On the Internet, nobody knows you're a dog." Not everyone is who they claim to be, and people can easily portray themselves however they would like. Someone who is self-employed, for example, may describe himself as a CEO on his LinkedIn profile.

If, while surfing on the internet, you come across a person whom you would like to meet, make sure his business has a website, working phone number, verifiable company data, and some degree of transparency. Meeting people online requires a little research, some discretion, and a lot of common sense. I recommend trying to network via local contacts first before trying the internet, and even then you should meet in a public place, such as a restaurant or coffee shop, to avoid bringing a total stranger into your place of work or home. Keep in mind that chemistry between you and potential team members is just as important as their individual skills and talents. Before you consider starting a business relationship with someone, you should feel absolutely comfortable with that person. The internet can help you ferret out what's going on in town—the business networks that are open to newcomers and the service clubs that are the most active—but nothing can replace face-to-face meetings as a way of getting to know someone on a more personal level.

If you are uncomfortable with approaching and conversing with others in this manner, it is essential that you find someone who can do it for or with you. Remember, you do not have to go to meetings alone. Perhaps the first person whose help you should seek is not a marketer or financial manager, but rather a business mentor or friend who can help you socialize and network with other professionals.

CONCLUSION

As I have said many times before, whatever you do, do not remain isolated. Contrary to popular belief, entrepreneurs must be social if they want to succeed. "Magical helpers" are out there, but only when you are truly committed to your idea and are determined to succeed. These are the captivating qualities that will attract people to you as an entrepreneur. Business networking is not unlike trying to find a job, or even someone to date and eventually marry. With this in mind, you should always be sincere when meeting potential members of your business team. Tell them about what you love to do—passion is contagious! Above all, do not claim to be good at everything, because no one wants to work for a know-it-all. Besides, the whole point of finding a team is precisely because you are not—and cannot—be good at everything. And when you believe you have found the right product person, marketer, or financial manager to help your company, allow him to tell you how he can contribute. Don't be quick to dismiss someone just because he does not entirely agree with you. The best business teams are made up of talented individuals with different opinions, and who see the world in different ways. The combined, multifaceted vision of the team can accomplish much more than any one person alone.

Conclusion

*"It was the best of times,
it was the worst of times . . ."*
—CHARLES DICKENS, *A TALE OF TWO CITIES*

I n light of today's great economic difficulties, these are certainly some of the "worst of times" that our generation has faced. Although the digital age has ushered in a new wave of cutting-edge technology that has improved our lives in many ways, there are still challenges in front of us. Every day, we are confronted with the daunting fact that we must feed, clothe, transport, heal, and educate 7 billion people in a sustainable way. The energy crisis alone is enough to keep the industry's leaders busy for the next century as they try to move us from smokestacks to "green" stacks. All of these challenges require great courage and ingenuity. So, while it may be the worst of times for many, it can be the *best* of times for entrepreneurs.

History has shown that the accomplishments of entrepreneurs are often unforeseen. In 1860, for example, experts believed that New York City would no longer exist by 1960 because they thought it would be impossible to accommodate its ever increasing population. They estimated that, by that time, the city's transportation needs would require approximately 6 million horses, which seemed simply unsustainable.

They never considered the possibility that a new means of transportation would become available. But by 1900, there were over a thousand automobile manufacturers in the United States. Thanks to forward-thinking entrepreneurs, the automobile was an overwhelming success. These industry pioneers did not know it at the time, but their combined efforts started a revolution. In their private stables and garages they produced the "horseless carriage" and moved forward from there, striving to meet market needs and desires. Although not every single entrepreneur achieved long-term success, together they transformed the world.

Entrepreneurs play a significant role in shaping the future. Especially in difficult economic times, the determination and drive of entrepreneurs gives us all reason to be optimistic. The challenges are great, but the individuals who are ultimately successful are those who remain committed to their goal. They take the steps necessary to make their dreams come true and, no matter how big or small their companies, they help to grow the economy and improve our way of life.

It isn't just the high-tech corporations that have an impact on the economic future. Small "mom and pop" operations are equally if not more important than large enterprises. The late Peter Drucker, a management consultant and writer, once said that while high-tech companies may comprise the *top* of the business world "mountain," the mountain itself is made up of millions of small and midsize companies. In fact, according to the US Small Business Administration, small businesses make up more than 99.7 percent of all employers and have generated 65 percent of new jobs over the past seventeen years. In other words, as a current or soon-to-be small business owner, you are contributing to the wealth of nations and fueling the economy.

We maintain that you will not succeed if you try to run your business by yourself. The phrase "lack of management" is often cited as the main reason for business failure. What this vague term actually means, though, is the lack of a *team*. A business team ensures that the key areas of a company are managed with skill, efficiency, and passion. My work with entrepreneurs has taught me that, regardless of the industry, work environment, or culture, the leading cause of business failure is solitude. If you stay in business alone, you are getting in the way of your own success. As journalist and best-selling author Malcolm Gladwell has argued, "No one—not rock stars, not professional athletes, not software billionaires, and not even geniuses—ever makes it alone." After all, one person cannot possibly fulfill every role in a business, which requires multiple skills, talents, passions, and personalities in order to run efficiently and keep afloat. This is precisely why the Trinity of Management works so well for companies. It is a business model based on a team approach, but its underlying philosophy acknowledges the importance of individual passion and talent. Furthermore, it recognizes that it is the combined effort of many people, not just one brilliant idea, that drives the success of a business.

Hopefully, you have figured out your role in the Trinity of Management and are ready to begin the process of finding the most qualified, committed individuals to complete your business team. Keep in mind that the best environment for you, as a current or future business owner, is not necessarily a classroom, but a nurturing community in which both social and professional networks are within easy reach. Mentoring, networking, supporting, and connecting are as vital to business success as individual passion, and entrepreneurial coaches, instructors, and facilitators should emphasize the social aspect of business formation. This will help to prevent small businesses from failing, as well as restore entrepreneurs to their central position in economic growth.

I wrote this book because I want to help entrepreneurs like you start successful businesses or transform the ones they already have. And if there is one piece of advice that I hope stays with you, it is that you will not succeed if you stay isolated. Solitude is the death of the entrepreneur. Just as you must look inward to understand your passion, you must look outward to find others to help you. Success in business rests primarily on these two actions. Never be reluctant or embarrassed to seek assistance, and do so with prudence and optimism. Remember, there are "magical helpers" out there waiting for a passionate "hero" to commit to the entrepreneurial journey. With their help and your own commitment, this can be the best of times for you and your business.

Appendix

Creating a Blueprint for Your Business

Preparing a business plan can be a complicated and overwhelming process for one person, which is why it's ideal to put a team together before you start to write it. Even a basic plan requires a broad knowledge base and skill set, which are rarely found in a single individual. Yet, you should not avoid creating a business plan simply because of the difficulty involved. Starting a business is a serious endeavor, and a business plan can serve as a helpful blueprint for your company. As an entrepreneur, you should be able to look into the future and face what lies ahead for your business. Whether you intend to present your plan to potential investors, or use it as a general guide for running your company, I suggest that you—preferably with the help of your team—begin to flesh out your business idea using the following ten-part template:

1. Cover sheet
2. Executive summary
3. Table of contents
4. Description of product or service
5. Industry analysis
6. Competitive analysis
7. Marketing and sales strategy
8. Operations

9. Management

10. Financial data

To give you a better idea of what information you should include in each part, explanations of the different sections are provided below.

- **Executive summary.** Approximately one to two pages in length, the executive summary is the first part of the business plan, placed between the cover sheet and the table of contents. The executive summary, which highlights the main points of your plan, should be straightforward, concise, and convincing so that it lures in the reader. The executive summary states the name and location of the business, the product or service sold, and the plan's purpose. It also presents key financial data, such as projected sales and profits. Although the executive summary appears first, it is usually written after you have drafted the plan in its entirety and therefore know its most important aspects.

- **Description of the product or service.** This section describes the specific item(s) your business will sell or the service it will provide, and distinguishes it from other products or services currently on the market. In other words, it explains the advantages of your product or service and how customers can benefit from it. It should also mention if you plan to offer additional products or services in the future. If the product or service is brand new to the marketplace, or if it involves technology of any kind, the description should be detailed. The total length of this section depends on the complexity of the product or service being sold. For example, if you are starting an auto parts business, you do not have to list every single car part, but rather provide a general, three- or four-page overview of the different part categories.

- **Industry analysis.** This part of the plan, which should be between one and three pages in length, addresses the various forces at work in your industry and how your company will fit into the "big picture." This analysis should cover the industry's past, present, and projected trends; employment patterns; and any growth or decline it has experienced over the decade or so. You may also want to mention if there are regulations or other factors that affect the industry, and how your company plans to overcome them.

- **Competitive analysis.** One of the most important elements of a business plan, the purpose of the competitive analysis is to demonstrate a clear and realistic understanding of your business's main competition. To write an accurate, comprehensive competitive analysis, some research is involved. The ideal person to gather information about your competitors is the marketer, who should assess strengths and weaknesses of competing businesses, and determine your company's competitive edge—the qualities that give it an advantage and make it stand out. If you are opening a restaurant, for instance, mention if you offer different menu options or lower prices. In addition, if your business sells a product that can be purchased easily online, you need to make a convincing case for buying the product directly from your company instead. This section can be anywhere from one to four pages in length.

- **Marketing and sales strategy.** The description of a company's marketing and sales strategy is one of the cornerstones of a business plan. Having a solid plan for advertising, promoting, and selling your product or service is essential for ensuring your business's viability, as well as convincing potential investors or lenders of its success. This section, which is usually between five and ten pages, must identify the target market and provide data to support its interest in or use for whatever you are selling. The person who writes this section—preferably the marketer—should also state the message that you wish to convey to customers about your product or service, and how this message will be communicated. For example, will your company use print media, websites, TV and radio, social media, trade shows, or a combination of these? Finally, this section should specify your business's intended channels of distribution, and how you will measure the effectiveness of its marketing and selling efforts.

- **Operations.** The operations section, which explains how the business is actually run, involves specific details and, therefore, should be carefully thought out before it is written. This part of the plan should answer questions such as: Where do you get your inventory, and how do you transport it to your business's location? Do customers come to you for the product or service, or do you go to them? Is the business transaction immediate, or do you invoice clients? If your business involves a manufacturing process, supplies, equipment, or facilities, this is the place where they should be described. In its entirety, this section can span two to five pages, depending on the complexity of the business operation. Since this will be dry reading, it's best to keep it to a few pages at most.

- **Management.** This section, which introduces the management team and staff, is particularly important to include if you intend to present your plan to potential stakeholders. In fact, it is one of the first parts that investors and lenders read, since they are usually interested in learning about the people in whom they may be investing. You should include background information on all the key members of your team in this section. Remember, *people*, not ideas, are the foundation of businesses, so this section is critical, and you should put your best foot forward. With that being said, be careful not to overdo it. Include only relevant details about a person's credentials and experience—this is not the place to list hobbies or personal information! Aim to limit your management section to about two pages.

- **Financial data.** This part of your plan must demonstrate the financial feasibility of your business. At minimum, it should include the following items:
  - Capital equipment and supply list (the equipment and supplies you use in producing, manufacturing, delivering, or selling your product or service)
  - Balance sheet
  - Break-even analysis
  - Profit and loss statements (summarize the revenues, costs, and expenses of a company over a certain period of time)

- Financial projections: (1) three-year summary; (2) detailed monthly projections for the first year; (3) detailed quarterly projections for the second and third years
- Assumptions upon which the financial projections are based
- Pro forma cash flow (a prediction of the flow of money in and out of a business over a given period of time)

It's absolutely crucial that you include this documentation, as most investors tend to read the financial section first. After all, they want assurance that they will make their money back—and then some. At the same time, though, this section is highly useful for you and your team, since it can serve as a short- and medium-term guide for running the company.

In addition to the sections described here, a business plan meant to be read by investors for the purpose of raising capital should include the items listed below.

- **Additional financial data, including an independent audit report.** If you are showing your plan to investors, be prepared to include tax returns of all business partners for the last three years. In addition, an independent audit report verifying all of the plan's financial data should be prepared by a reputable accounting firm and included as an attached document. Ideally, the financial data contained in the plan should reflect a willingness to minimize the company's risks by starting small, but also clearly demonstrate an expansion pattern based on the fulfillment of its projected income. Furthermore, it should show that you and your team have invested your *own* money in the business, as this obviously indicates a strong level of commitment.

- **Business team credentials.** The individual backgrounds and qualifications of the business team members should be described in the Management section of the business plan. They should also be verbally mentioned at the meeting with investors, preferably during the introductions. Team members need to make their qualifications apparent to investors by being able to answer specific questions related to their areas of expertise.

- **Copies of licenses, patents, and other legal documents.** This documentation may pertain to the legal protection of the company's products and other intellectual property. A copy of the proposed lease or purchase agreement for the company's building or office space is also required.

- **Letters of intent to purchase.** As explained in Chapter 8 (see page 83), these are letters from potential clients expressing interest in your product or service, as well as their intention to buy it once it is available. Letters of intent to purchase demonstrate that your company has done the necessary market research, and that your product or service has market acceptance. The letters should be placed in the marketing section of your business plan.

In general, a business plan demonstrating that you have an interesting, cost-effective product that can be protected, marketed, and sold is a valuable tool for jumpstarting your business. And when you have a highly qualified, dedicated team in place, you will also have a very good chance of attracting investors.

Depending on the nature of your business, your business plan may require more complex information. But like riding a bicycle, expanding and refining a business plan becomes easier when the process is already in motion. In other words, building your business plan is less difficult if you already have the blueprint. There are also plenty of books and websites that offer helpful advice for writing a more detailed business plan. I recommend *Business Plans That Win $$$: Lessons from the MIT Enterprise Forum* by Stanley R. Rich and David E. Gumpert, a book that has been one of the best resources for entrepreneurs for many years. I also suggest visiting web pages available through the MIT and Harvard Business School websites (http://web.mit.edu/e-club/hadzima/ and http://www.hbs.edu/entrepreneurship/), which provide useful information and additional resources for entrepreneurs.

References

Introduction

1. de Botton, Alain. *The Pleasures and Sorrows of Work*. New York: Vintage Books, 2009.

1. Why Some Entrepreneurs Succeed While Others Fail

1. Page, Dan. "UCLA Team Maps How Genes Affect Brain Structure, Intelligence; Dramatic Images Shed Light on Brain Diseases, Personality Differences." *UCLA Newsroom*. November 4, 2001. Accessed August 20, 2011 http://newsroom.ucla.edu/portal/ucla/UCLA-Team-Maps-How-Genes-Affect-2820.aspx.

2. The Trinity of Management

1. McCallum, Jack. "Mission Impossible." *Sports Illustrated,* November 6, 1989. Accessed October 10, 2011. http://sportsillustrated.cnn.com/si_on line/flashbacks/jordan/891106.

2. Sachare, Alex. "Reliving the Pistons-Bulls Rivalry." *NBA.com,* March 12, 2003. Accessed October 10, 2011. http://www.nba.com/pistons/history/bullsrivalry_030314.html.

6. Six Common Misconceptions About Business

1. Roxburgh, Charles, Susan Lund, and John Piotrowski. "Mapping Global Capital Markets, 2011." McKinsey Global Institute, August 2011.

9. The Social Aspect of Entrepreneurship

1. Davidsson, Per. "Looking Back at 20 Years of Entrepreneurship Research: What Did We Learn?" *Entrepreneurship, Sustainable Growth and Performance: Frontiers in European Entrepreneurship Research*, edited by Hans Landström, Hans Crijns, Eddy Laveren, and David Smallbone, 13–26. Cheltenham, UK: Edward Elgar Publishing, 2008.

2. Davidsson, Per and Benson Honig. "The Role of Social and Human Capital Among Nascent Entrepreneurs." *Journal of Business Venturing* 18, no. 3 (2003): 301–331.

3. Sarasvathy, Saras D. "Causation and Effectuation: Toward a Theoretical Shift from Economic Inevitability to Entrepreneurial Contingency." *Academy of Management Review* 26, no. 2 (2001): 243–263.

About the Author

Dr. Ernesto Sirolli received a Laurea di Dottore in Political Science from Rome University and a PhD in Philosophy from Murdoch University in Perth, Australia. For over thirty years, he has worked in the US, Canada, Mexico, Europe, Africa, Australia, South America, and New Zealand in the field of local economic development. In 1984, he pioneered a novel approach to local development based on "facilitating" the transformation of local good ideas into viable businesses. By the following year, Ernesto had turned this concept into Enterprise Facilitation®, a model of local development which has since been implemented in hundreds of communities all over the world.

Dr. Sirolli is the founder of Sirolli Institute International, a social enterprise based in Sacramento, California, as well as an adjunct professor at the Norman B. Keevil Institute at the University of British Columbia. He is also the bestselling author of *Ripples from the Zambezi: Passion, Entrepreneurship, and the Rebirth of Local Economies* and a highly sought-after speaker who gives lectures worldwide, as well as trains others in Enterprise Facilitation and the Trinity of Management.

About the
Sirolli Institute

The Sirolli Institute is a non-profit social organization dedicated to Enterprise Facilitation®, an innovative method of local economic development based on capturing and channeling the entrepreneurial spirit of local communities. The Institute also teaches entrepreneurs the Trinity of Management, a team approach to business management. Finally, the Sirolli Institute consults with development and mining companies in the field of corporate social responsibility, advising them on how to create sustainable economic cooperation within the communities they affect.

For more information on the Sirolli Institute, please visit www.sirolli.com, call 1-800-SIROLLI, or follow @sirollinstitute on Twitter.

Index

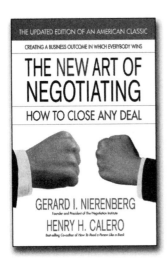

THE UPDATED EDITION OF AN AMERICAN CLASSIC

CREATING A BUSINESS OUTCOME IN WHICH EVERYBODY WINS

THE NEW ART OF NEGOTIATING

HOW TO CLOSE ANY DEAL

GERARD I. NIERENBERG
Founder and President of The Negotiation Institute

HENRY H. CALERO
Best-selling Co-author of How To Read a Person Like a Book

THE NEW ART OF NEGOTIATING

How to Close Any Deal

Gerard I. Nierenberg and Henry H. Calero

You negotiate every day of your life. Whether you are closing a business deal, asking your employer for a raise, or simply persuading your child to do his homework, everything is a negotiation. Written by Gerard Nierenberg and Henry Calero, world-renowned experts in the field, *The New Art of Negotiating* introduces you to the many crucial skills involved in effective negotiation.

Early in their careers, Nierenberg and Calero made a revolutionary discovery: Negotiation does not have to be an adversarial process that ends in victory for one party and defeat for the other. By having a clear understanding of each party's goals, you can steer clear of the common obstacles that derail most deals. *The New Art of Negotiating* provides the authors' proven strategies for avoiding these pitfalls in our fast-changing, high-pressured world. You will learn how to analyze your opponent's motivation, negotiate toward mutually satisfying terms, learn from your opponent's body language, and much more. Throughout, the authors will guide you in successfully applying their famous "everybody wins" tactics.

Gerard Nierenberg and Henry Calero have changed the way we think about negotiating, elevating the process to an exciting new level. With *The New Art of Negotiating,* you can control your own destiny and experience win-win success in today's challenging business and social climate.

$15.95 US • 256 pages • 6 x 9-inch quality paperback • ISBN 978-0-7570-0305-9

HOW TO READ A PERSON LIKE A BOOK

Observing Body Language to Know What People Are Thinking

Gerard I. Nierenberg, Henry H. Calero, and Gabriel Grayson

Imagine meeting someone for the first time and within minutes—without a word being said—having the ability to tell what that person is thinking. Magic? Not quite. Whether people are aware of it or not, their body movements clearly express their attitudes and motives. These simple gestures, which most of us don't even notice, can communicate key information that is invaluable in a range of situations.

How to Read a Person Like a Book is designed to teach you how to interpret and respond to the nonverbal signals of business associates, friends, loved ones, and even strangers. Best-selling authors Gerard Nierenberg, Henry Calero, and Gabriel Grayson have collaborated to put their working knowledge of body language into this practical guide to recognizing, understanding, and using nonverbal communication. With *How to Read a Person Like a Book,* you will learn:

☐ How to tell if someone is not being truthful.

☐ When to push forward or back off during a negotiation.

☐ How to identify an aggressive or submissive handshake.

☐ When someone has lost interest in what you are saying.

☐ How to put people at ease by mirroring their gestures.

☐ Why your body language can make or break a deal.

Whether in an office, on a date, or on a family outing, the simple technique of reading body language is a unique skill that offers real and important benefits.

$13.95 US • 128 pages • 6 x 9-inch quality paperback • ISBN 978-0-7570-0314-1

INVESTIGATIVE SELLING

How to Master the Art, Science & Skills of Professional Selling

Omar Periu

Within each super salesperson is an expert detective who is every bit as skilled as any Sherlock Holmes, Hercule Poirot, or Nero Wolfe. For a lucky few, these sleuthing talents come naturally. For most, however, these skills must be learned, practiced, and refined—and it is this set of skills that turns the average salesperson into the master seller. Now, Omar Periu, nationally renowned "high energy" sales trainer and master salesman, provides readers with the secrets of becoming a top sales professional in his comprehensive book *Investigative Selling*.

Like any good investigation, selling begins with observation, questioning, and listening. What you look for, how you ask your questions, and what you hear can provide you with all the clues you need to seal that important sale. *Investigative Selling* not only details these important skills, but also explains the most effective way to use the information you gather. And it applies investigative selling techniques to a range of sales activities, from prospecting to qualifying, from presenting to closing. Throughout the book, simple icons help you identify the recommended strategy, and important tips and tactics are clearly highlighted so that you don't miss a trick.

Where do you stand now in your sales career? Could your skills be improved? Are you happy with your sales figures? Are you satisfied with the money you're making? If the answers make you uncomfortable, this is the "how to" book you need to read now.

$15.95 US • 240 pages • 6 x 9-inch quality paperback • ISBN 978-0-7570-0285-4

**For more information about our books,
visit our website at www.squareonepublishers.com**